5/6

27p

THE PLAYS OF TCHEHOV

VOL. I.

THE CHERRY ORCHARD

AND OTHER PLAYS

TRANSLATED BY CONSTANCE GARNETT

THE TALES OF ANTON TCHEHOV

St Martin's Library Edition. Pott 8vo. Cloth and leather

I. The Darling, & other Stories
II. The Duel, &c.
III. The Lady with the Dog, &c.
IV. The Party, &c.
V. The Wife, &c.
VI. The Witch, &c.
VII. The Bishop, &c.
VIII. The Chorus Girl, &c.
IX. The Schoolmistress, &c.
X. The Horse-stealers, &c.
XI. The Schoolmaster, &c.
XII. The Cook's Wedding, &c.
XIII. Love, &c.

THE PLAYS OF ANTON TCHEHOV

St Martin's Library Edition. Pott 8vo. Cloth and leather

I. The Cherry Orchard, & other Plays
II. Three Sisters, &c.

LETTERS OF ANTON TCHEHOV

With a biographical introduction and 8 portraits.
Demy 8vo.

LETTERS OF ANTON TCHEHOV TO OLGA KNIPPER

With Preface by Olga Knipper
Demy 8vo.

THE CHERRY ORCHARD

AND OTHER PLAYS

BY

ANTON TCHEHOV

FROM THE RUSSIAN

BY CONSTANCE GARNETT

LONDON
CHATTO & WINDUS
1926

PRINTED IN ENGLAND
AT THE BALLANTYNE PRESS
SPOTTISWOODE, BALLANTYNE & CO. LTD.
COLCHESTER, LONDON
& ETON

ALL RIGHTS STRICTLY
RESERVED

First published, April 1923
Reprinted 1925 *and* 1926

CONTENTS

THE CHERRY ORCHARD

A COMEDY IN FOUR ACTS

First performed at Moscow,
January 17, 1904

CHARACTERS IN THE PLAY

MADAME RANEVSKY (LYUBOV ANDREYEVNA) (*the owner of the Cherry Orchard*).
ANYA (*her daughter, aged* 17).
VARYA (*her adopted daughter, aged* 24).
GAEV (LEONID ANDREYEVITCH) (*brother of Madame Ranevsky*).
LOPAHIN (YERMOLAY ALEXEYEVITCH) (*a Merchant*).
TROFIMOV (PYOTR SERGEYEVITCH) (*a Student*).
SEMYONOV-PISHTCHIK (*a Landowner*).
CHARLOTTA IVANOVNA (*a Governess*).
EPIHODOV (SEMYON PANTALEYEVITCH) *a Clerk*).
DUNYASHA (*a Maid*).
FIRS (*an old Valet, aged* 87).
YASHA (*a young Valet*).
A VAGRANT.
THE STATION MASTER.
A POST-OFFICE CLERK.
VISITORS, SERVANTS.

The action takes place on the estate of MADAME RANEVSKY.

ACT I

A room, which has always been called the nursery. One of the doors leads into ANYA'S *room. Dawn, sun rises during the scene. May, the cherry trees in flower, but it is cold in the garden with the frost of early morning. Windows closed.*

Enter DUNYASHA *with a candle and* LOPAHIN *with a book in his hand.*

LOPAHIN. The train's in, thank God. What time is it ?

DUNYASHA. Nearly two o'clock (*puts out the candle*). It's daylight already.

LOPAHIN. The train's late ! Two hours, at least (*yawns and stretches*). I'm a pretty one ; what a fool I've been. Came here on purpose to meet them at the station and dropped asleep. . . . Dozed off as I sat in the chair. It's annoying. . . . You might have waked me.

DUNYASHA. I thought you had gone (*listens*). There, I do believe they're coming !

LOPAHIN (*listens*). No, what with the luggage and one thing and another (*a pause*). Lyubov Andreyevna has been abroad five years ; I don't know what she is like now. . . . She's a splendid woman. A good-natured, kind-hearted woman. I remember when I was a lad of fifteen, my poor father—he used to keep a little shop here in the village in those days—gave me a punch in the face with his fist and made my nose bleed. We were in the yard here, I forget what we'd come about—he had had a drop. Lyubov Andreyevna—I can see her now—she was a slim young girl then—took me to wash my face, and then brought me into this very room, into the nursery. "Don't cry, little peasant," says she, "it will be well in time for your wedding day" . . . (*a pause*). Little peasant. . . . My father was a peasant, it's true, but here am I in a white waistcoat and brown shoes, like a pig in a bun shop. Yes, I'm a rich man, but for all my money, come to think, a peasant I was, and a peasant I am (*turns over the pages of the book*). I've been reading this book and I can't make head or tail of it. I fell asleep over it (*a pause*).

DUNYASHA. The dogs have been awake all night, they feel that the mistress is coming.

LOPAHIN. Why, what's the matter with you, Dunyasha?

DUNYASHA. My hands are all of a tremble. I feel as though I should faint.

LOPAHIN. You're a spoilt soft creature, Dunyasha. And dressed like a lady too, and your hair done up. That's not the thing. One must know one's place.

(*Enter* EPIHODOV *with a nosegay; he wears a pea-jacket and highly polished creaking top-boots; he drops the nosegay as he comes in.*)

EPIHODOV (*picking up the nosegay*). Here! the gardener's sent this, says you're to put it in the dining-room (*gives* DUNYASHA *the nosegay*).

LOPAHIN. And bring me some kvass.

DUNYASHA. I will (*goes out*).

EPIHODOV. It's chilly this morning, three degrees of frost, though the cherries are all in flower. I can't say much for our climate (*sighs*). I can't. Our climate is not often propitious to the occasion. Yermolay Alexeyevitch, permit me to call your attention to the fact that I purchased myself a pair of boots the day before yesterday, and they creak, I venture to assure you, so that there's no tolerating them. What ought I to grease them with ?

LOPAHIN. Oh, shut up ! Don't bother me.

EPIHODOV. Every day some misfortune befalls me. I don't complain, I'm used to it, and I wear a smiling face.

(DUNYASHA *comes in, hands* LOPAHIN *the kvass.*)

EPIHODOV. I am going (*stumbles against a chair, which falls over*). There ! (*as though triumphant*). There you see now, excuse the expression, an accident like that among others. . . . It's positively remarkable (*goes out*).

DUNYASHA. Do you know, Yermolay Alexeyevitch, I must confess, Epihodov has made me a proposal.

LOPAHIN. Ah !

DUNYASHA. I'm sure I don't know. . . . He's a harmless fellow, but sometimes when he begins talking, there's no making anything of it. It's all very fine and expressive, only there's no understanding it. I've a sort of liking for him too. He loves me to distraction. He's an unfortunate man; every day there's something. They tease him about it—two and twenty misfortunes they call him.

LOPAHIN (*listening*). There! I do believe they're coming.

DUNYASHA. They *are* coming! What's the matter with me? . . . I'm cold all over.

LOPAHIN. They really are coming. Let's go and meet them. Will she know me? It's five years since I saw her.

DUNYASHA (*in a flutter*). I shall drop this very minute. . . . Ah, I shall drop.

(*There is a sound of two carriages driving up to the house.* LOPAHIN *and* DUNYASHA *go out quickly. The stage is left empty. A noise is heard in the adjoining rooms.* FIRS, *who has driven to meet* MADAME RANEVSKY, *crosses the stage hurriedly leaning on a stick. He is wearing old-fashioned livery and a high hat. He says something to himself, but not a word can be distinguished. The noise behind the scenes goes on increasing. A voice: "Come, let's go in here." Enter* LYUBOV ANDREYEVNA, ANYA, *and* CHARLOTTA IVANOVNA *with a pet dog on a chain, all in travelling dresses,* VARYA *in an out-door coat with a kerchief over her head,* GAEV, SEMYONOV-PISHTCHIK, LOPAHIN, DUNYASHA *with bag and parasol, servants with other articles. All walk across the room.*)

ANYA. Let's come in here. Do you remember what room this is, mamma?

LYUBOV (*joyfully, through her tears*). The nursery!

VARYA. How cold it is, my hands are numb. (*To* LYUBOV ANDREYEVNA) Your rooms, the white room and the lavender one, are just the same as ever, mamma.

LYUBOV. My nursery, dear delightful room. . . . I used to sleep here when I was little . . . (*cries*). And here I am, like a little child . . . (*kisses her brother and* VARYA, *and then her brother again*). Varya's just the same as ever, like a nun. And I knew Dunyasha (*kisses* DUNYASHA).

GAEV. The train was two hours late. What do you think of that? Is that the way to do things?

CHARLOTTA (*to* PISHTCHIK). My dog eats nuts, too.

PISHTCHIK (*wonderingly*). Fancy that!

(*They all go out except* ANYA *and* DUNYASHA.)

DUNYASHA. We've been expecting you so long (*takes* ANYA'S *hat and coat*).

ANYA. I haven't slept for four nights on the journey. I feel dreadfully cold.

DUNYASHA. You set out in Lent, there was snow and frost, and now? My darling! (*laughs and kisses her*). I *have* missed you, my precious, my joy. I must tell you . . . I can't put it off a minute. . . .

ANYA (*wearily*). What now?

DUNYASHA. Epihodov, the clerk, made me a proposal just after Easter.

ANYA. It's always the same thing with you . . . (*straightening her hair*). I've lost all my hairpins . . . (*she is staggering from exhaustion*).

DUNYASHA. I don't know what to think, really. He does love me, he does love me so!

ANYA (*looking towards her door, tenderly*). My own room, my windows just as though I had never gone away. I'm home! To-morrow morning I shall get up and run into the garden. . . . Oh, if I could get to sleep! I haven't slept all the journey, I was so anxious and worried.

DUNYASHA. Pyotr Sergeyevitch came the day before yesterday.

ANYA (*joyfully*). Petya!

DUNYASHA. He's asleep in the bath house, he has settled in there. I'm afraid of being in their way, says he. (*Glancing at her watch*) I was to have waked him, but Varvara Mihalovna told me not to. Don't you wake him, says she.

(*Enter* VARYA *with a bunch of keys at her waist.*)

VARYA. Dunyasha, coffee and make haste. . . . Mamma's asking for coffee.

DUNYASHA. This very minute (*goes out*).

VARYA. Well, thank God, you've come. You're home again (*petting her*). My little darling has come back! My precious beauty has come back again!

ANYA. I have had a time of it!

VARYA. I can fancy!

ANYA. We set off in Holy Week—it was so cold then, and all the way Charlotta would talk and show off her tricks. What did you want to burden me with Charlotta for?

VARYA. You couldn't have travelled all alone, darling. At seventeen!

ANYA. We got to Paris at last, it was cold there

—snow. I speak French shockingly. Mamma lives on the fifth floor, I went up to her, and there were a lot of French people, ladies, an old priest with a book. The place smelt of tobacco and so comfortless. I felt sorry, oh! so sorry for mamma all at once, I put my arms round her neck, and hugged her and wouldn't let her go. Mamma was as kind as she could be, and she cried. . . .

VARYA (*through her tears*). Don't speak of it, don't speak of it!

ANYA. She had sold her villa at Mentone, she had nothing left, nothing. I hadn't a farthing left either, we only just had enough to get here. And mamma doesn't understand! When we had dinner at the stations, she always ordered the most expensive things and gave the waiters a whole rouble. Charlotta's just the same. Yasha too must have the same as we do; it's simply awful. You know Yasha is mamma's valet now, we brought him here with us.

VARYA. Yes, I've seen the young rascal.

ANYA. Well, tell me—have you paid the arrears on the mortgage?

VARYA. How could we get the money?

ANYA. Oh, dear! Oh, dear!

VARYA. In August the place will be sold.

ANYA. My goodness!

LOPAHIN (*peeps in at the door and moo's like a cow*). Moo! (*disappears*).

VARYA (*weeping*). There, that's what I could do to him (*shakes her fist*).

ANYA (*embracing* VARYA, *softly*). Varya, has he made you an offer? (VARYA *shakes her head.*)

Why, but he loves you. Why is it you don't come to an understanding? What are you waiting for?

VARYA. I believe that there never will be anything between us. He has a lot to do, he has no time for me . . . and takes no notice of me. Bless the man, it makes me miserable to see him. . . . Everyone's talking of our being married, everyone's congratulating me, and all the while there's really nothing in it; it's all like a dream. (*In another tone*) You have a new brooch like a bee.

ANYA (*mournfully*). Mamma bought it. (*Goes into her own room and in a light-hearted childish tone*) And you know, in Paris I went up in a balloon!

VARYA. My darling's home again! My pretty is home again!

(DUNYASHA *returns with the coffee-pot and is making the coffee.*)

VARYA (*standing at the door*). All day long, darling, as I go about looking after the house, I keep dreaming all the time. If only we could marry you to a rich man, then I should feel more at rest. Then I would go off by myself on a pilgrimage to Kiev, to Moscow . . . and so I would spend my life going from one holy place to another. . . . I would go on and on. . . . What bliss!

ANYA. The birds are singing in the garden. What time is it?

VARYA. It must be nearly three. It's time you were asleep, darling (*going into* ANYA'S *room*). What bliss!

(YASHA *enters with a rug and a travelling bag.*)

YASHA (*crosses the stage, mincingly*). May one come in here, pray?

DUNYASHA. I shouldn't have known you, Yasha. How you have changed abroad.

YASHA. H'm! . . . And who are you?

DUNYASHA. When you went away, I was that high (*shows distance from floor*). Dunyasha, Fyodor's daughter. . . . You don't remember me!

YASHA. H'm! . . . You're a peach! (*looks round and embraces her: she shrieks and drops a saucer.* YASHA *goes out hastily*).

VARYA (*in the doorway, in a tone of vexation*). What now?

DUNYASHA (*through her tears*). I have broken a saucer.

VARYA. Well, that brings good luck.

ANYA (*coming out of her room*). We ought to prepare mamma: Petya is here.

VARYA. I told them not to wake him.

ANYA (*dreamily*). It's six years since father died. Then only a month later little brother Grisha was drowned in the river, such a pretty boy he was, only seven. It was more than mamma could bear, so she went away, went away without looking back (*shuddering*). . . . How well I understand her, if only she knew! (*a pause*) And Petya Trofimov was Grisha's tutor, he may remind her.

(*Enter* FIRS: *he is wearing a pea-jacket and a white waistcoat.*)

FIRS (*goes up to the coffee-pot, anxiously*). The mistress will be served here (*puts on white gloves*). Is the coffee ready? (*Sternly to* DUNYASHA) Girl! Where's the cream?

DUNYASHA. Ah, mercy on us! (*goes out quickly*).

FIRS (*fussing round the coffee-pot*). Ech! you good-for-nothing! (*muttering to himself*). Come back from Paris. And the old master used to go to Paris too . . . horses all the way (*laughs*).

VARYA. What is it, Firs?

FIRS. What is your pleasure? (*Gleefully*) My lady has come home! I have lived to see her again! Now I can die (*weeps with joy*).

(*Enter* LYUBOV ANDREYEVNA, GAEV *and* SEMYONOV-PISHTCHIK; *the latter is in a short-waisted full coat of fine cloth, and full trousers.* GAEV, *as he comes in, makes a gesture with his arms and his whole body, as though he were playing billiards.*)

LYUBOV. How does it go? Let me remember. Cannon off the red!

GAEV. That's it—in off the white! Why, once, sister, we used to sleep together in this very room, and now I'm fifty-one, strange as it seems.

LOPAHIN. Yes, time flies.

GAEV. What do you say?

LOPAHIN. Time, I say, flies.

GAEV. What a smell of patchouli!

ANYA. I'm going to bed. Good-night, mamma (*kisses her mother*).

LYUBOV. My precious darling (*kisses her hands*). Are you glad to be home? I can't believe it.

ANYA. Good-night, uncle.

GAEV (*kissing her face and hands*). God bless you! How like you are to your mother! (*To his sister*) At her age you were just the same, Lyuba.

(ANYA *shakes hands with* LOPAHIN *and* PISHTCHIK, *then goes out, shutting the door after her.*)

LYUBOV. She's quite worn out.

PISHTCHIK. Aye, it's a long journey, to be sure.

VARYA (*to* LOPAHIN *and* PISHTCHIK). Well, gentlemen? It's three o'clock and time to say good-bye.

LYUBOV (*laughs*). You're just the same as ever, Varya (*draws her to her and kisses her*). I'll just drink my coffee and then we will all go and rest. (FIRS *puts a cushion under her feet.*) Thanks, friend. I am so fond of coffee, I drink it day and night. Thanks, dear old man (*kisses* FIRS).

VARYA. I'll just see whether all the things have been brought in (*goes out*).

LYUBOV. Can it really be me sitting here? (*laughs*). I want to dance about and clap my hands. (*Covers her face with her hands*) And I could drop asleep in a moment! God knows I love my country, I love it tenderly; I couldn't look out of the window in the train, I kept crying so. (*Through her tears*) But I must drink my coffee, though. Thank you, Firs, thanks, dear old man. I'm so glad to find you still alive.

FIRS. The day before yesterday.

GAEV. He's rather deaf.

LOPAHIN. I have to set off for Harkov directly, at five o'clock. . . . It is annoying! I wanted to have a look at you, and a little talk. . . . You are just as splendid as ever.

PISHTCHIK (*breathing heavily*). Handsomer,

indeed. . . . Dressed in Parisian style . . . completely bowled me over.

LOPAHIN. Your brother, Leonid Andreyevitch here, is always saying that I'm a low-born knave, that I'm a money-grubber, but I don't care one straw for that. Let him talk. Only I do want you to believe in me as you used to. I do want your wonderful tender eyes to look at me as they used to in the old days. Merciful God! My father was a serf of your father and of your grandfather, but you—you—did so much for me once, that I've forgotten all that; I love you as though you were my kin . . . more than my kin.

LYUBOV. I can't sit still, I simply can't . . . (*jumps up and walks about in violent agitation*). This happiness is too much for me. . . . You may laugh at me, I know I'm silly. . . . My own bookcase (*kisses the bookcase*). My little table.

GAEV. Nurse died while you were away.

LYUBOV (*sits down and drinks coffee*). Yes, the Kingdom of Heaven be hers! You wrote me of her death.

GAEV. And Anastasy is dead. Squinting Petrushka has left me and is in service now with the police captain in the town (*takes a box of caramels out of his pocket and sucks one*).

PISHTCHIK. My daughter, Dashenka, wishes to be remembered to you.

LOPAHIN. I want to tell you something very pleasant and cheering (*glancing at his watch*). I'm going directly . . . there's no time to say much . . . well, I can say it in a couple of words. I needn't tell you your cherry orchard is to be sold to pay your debts ; the 22nd of August is the date fixed for the sale ; but don't you worry, dearest lady, you may sleep in peace, there is a way of saving it. . . . This is what I propose. I beg your attention! Your estate is not twenty miles from the town, the railway runs close by it, and if the cherry orchard and the land along the river bank were cut up into building plots and then let on lease for summer villas, you would make an income of at least 25,000 roubles a year out of it.

GAEV. That's all rot, if you'll excuse me.

LYUBOV. I don't quite understand you, Yermolay Alexeyevitch.

LOPAHIN. You will get a rent of at least 25 roubles a year for a three-acre plot from summer visitors, and if you say the word now, I'll bet you what you like there won't be one square foot of ground vacant by the autumn, all the plots will be taken up. I congratulate you ; in fact, you are saved. It's a perfect situation with that deep river. Only, of course, it must be cleared—all the old buildings, for example, must be removed, this house too, which is really good for nothing, and the old cherry orchard must be cut down.

LYUBOV. Cut down? My dear fellow, forgive me, but you don't know what you are talking about. If there is one thing interesting—remarkable indeed—in the whole province, it's just our cherry orchard.

LOPAHIN. The only thing remarkable about the orchard is that it's a very large one. There's a crop of cherries every alternate year, and then there's nothing to be done with them, no one buys them.

GAEV. This orchard is mentioned in the 'Encyclopædia.'

LOPAHIN (*glancing at his watch*). If we don't decide on something and don't take some steps, on the 22nd of August the cherry orchard and the whole estate too will be sold by auction. Make up your minds! There is no other way of saving it, I'll take my oath on that. No, no!

FIRS. In old days, forty or fifty years ago, they used to dry the cherries, soak them, pickle them, make jam too, and they used——

GAEV. Be quiet, Firs.

FIRS. And they used to send the preserved cherries to Moscow and to Harkov by the waggon-load. That brought the money in! And the preserved cherries in those days were soft and juicy, sweet and fragrant. . . . They knew the way to do them then. . . .

LYUBOV. And where is the recipe now?

FIRS. It's forgotten. Nobody remembers it.

PISHTCHIK (*to* LYUBOV ANDREYEVNA). What's it like in Paris? Did you eat frogs there?

LYUBOV. Oh, I ate crocodiles.

PISHTCHIK. Fancy that now!

LOPAHIN. There used to be only the gentlefolks and the peasants in the country, but now there are these summer visitors. All the towns, even the small ones, are surrounded nowadays by these summer villas. And one may say for sure, that in another twenty years there'll be many more of these people and that they'll be everywhere. At present the summer visitor only drinks tea in his verandah, but maybe he'll take to working his bit of land too, and then your cherry orchard would become happy, rich and prosperous. . . .

GAEV (*indignant*). What rot!

(*Enter* VARYA *and* YASHA.)

VARYA. There are two telegrams for you, mamma (*takes out keys and opens an old-fashioned bookcase with a loud crack*). Here they are.

LYUBOV. From Paris (*tears the telegrams, without reading them*). I have done with Paris.

GAEV. Do you know, Lyuba, how old that bookcase is? Last week I pulled out the bottom drawer and there I found the date branded on it. The bookcase was made just a hundred years ago. What do you say to that? We might have celebrated its jubilee. Though it's an inanimate object, still it is a *book* case.

PISHTCHIK (*amazed*). A hundred years! Fancy that now.

GAEV. Yes. . . . It is a thing . . . (*feeling the bookcase*). Dear, honoured, bookcase! Hail to thee who for more than a hundred years hast served the pure ideals of good and justice; thy silent call to fruitful labour has never flagged in those hundred years, maintaining (*in tears*) in the generations of man, courage and faith in a brighter future and fostering in us ideals of good and social consciousness (*a pause*).

LOPAHIN. Yes. . . .

LYUBOV. You are just the same as ever, Leonid.

GAEV (*a little embarrassed*). Cannon off the right into the pocket!

LOPAHIN (*looking at his watch*). Well, it's time I was off.

YASHA (*handing* LYUBOV ANDREYEVNA *medicine*). Perhaps you will take your pills now.

PISHTCHIK. You shouldn't take medicines, my dear madam . . . they do no harm and no good. Give them here . . . honoured lady (*takes the pill-box, pours the pills into the hollow of his hand, blows on them, puts them in his mouth and drinks off some kvass*). There !

LYUBOV (*in alarm*). Why, you must be out of your mind !

PISHTCHIK. I have taken all the pills.

LOPAHIN. What a glutton ! (*All laugh.*)

FIRS. His honour stayed with us in Easter week, ate a gallon and a half of cucumbers . . . (*mutters*).

LYUBOV. What is he saying ?

VARYA. He has taken to muttering like that for the last three years. We are used to it.

YASHA. His declining years !

(CHARLOTTA IVANOVNA, *a very thin, lanky figure in a white dress with a lorgnette in her belt, walks across the stage.*)

LOPAHIN. I beg your pardon, Charlotta Ivanovna, I have not had time to greet you (*tries to kiss her hand*).

CHARLOTTA (*pulling away her hand*). If I let you kiss my hand, you'll be wanting to kiss my elbow, and then my shoulder.

LOPAHIN. I've no luck to-day ! (*All laugh.*) Charlotta Ivanovna, show us some tricks !

LYUBOV. Charlotta, do show us some tricks !

CHARLOTTA. I don't want to. I'm sleepy (*goes out*).

LOPAHIN. In three weeks' time we shall meet again (*kisses* LYUBOV ANDREYEVNA'S *hand*). Good-bye till then—I must go. (*To* GAEV) Good-bye. (*Kisses* PISHTCHIK) Good-bye. (*Gives his hand to* VARYA, *then to* FIRS *and* YASHA) I don't want to go. (*To* LYUBOV ANDREYEVNA) If you think over my plan for the villas and make up your mind, then let me know; I will lend you 50,000 roubles. Think of it seriously.

VARYA (*angrily*). Well, do go, for goodness sake.

LOPAHIN. I'm going, I'm going (*goes out*).

GAEV. Low-born knave! I beg pardon, though . . . Varya is going to marry him, he's Varya's fiancé.

VARYA. Don't talk nonsense, uncle.

LYUBOV. Well, Varya, I shall be delighted. He's a good man.

PISHTCHIK. He is, one must acknowledge, a most worthy man. And my Dashenka . . . says too that . . . she says . . . various things (*snores, but at once wakes up*). But all the same, honoured lady, could you oblige me . . . with a loan of 240 roubles . . . to pay the interest on my mortgage to-morrow?

VARYA (*dismayed*). No, no.

LYUBOV. I really haven't any money.

PISHTCHIK. It will turn up (*laughs*). I never lose hope. I thought everything was over, I was a ruined man, and lo and behold—the railway passed through my land and . . . they paid me for it. And something else will turn up again, if not to-day, then to-morrow . . . Dashenka'll win two hundred thousand . . . she's got a lottery ticket.

LYUBOV. Well, we've finished our coffee, we can go to bed.

FIRS (*brushes* GAEV, *reprovingly*). You have got on the wrong trousers again! What am I to do with you?

VARYA (*softly*). Anya's asleep. (*Softly opens the window*) Now the sun's risen, it's not a bit cold. Look, mamma, what exquisite trees! My goodness! And the air! The starlings are singing!

GAEV (*opens another window*). The orchard is all white. You've not forgotten it, Lyuba? That long avenue that runs straight, straight as an arrow, how it shines on a moonlight night. You remember? You've not forgotten?

LYUBOV (*looking out of the window into the garden*). Oh, my childhood, my innocence! It was in this nursery I used to sleep, from here I looked out into the orchard, happiness waked with me every morning and in those days the orchard was just the same, nothing has changed (*laughs with delight*). All, all white! Oh, my orchard! After the dark gloomy autumn, and the cold winter; you are young again, and full of happiness, the heavenly angels have never left you. . . . If I could cast off the burden that weighs on my heart, if I could forget the past!

GAEV. H'm! and the orchard will be sold to pay our debts; it seems strange. . . .

LYUBOV. See, our mother walking . . . all in white, down the avenue! (*laughs with delight*). It is she!

GAEV. Where?

VARYA. Oh, don't, mamma!

LYUBOV. There is no one. It was my fancy. On the right there, by the path to the arbour, there is a white tree bending like a woman. . . .

(*Enter* TROFIMOV *wearing a shabby student's uniform and spectacles.*)

LYUBOV. What a ravishing orchard! White masses of blossom, blue sky. . . .

TROFIMOV. Lyubov Andreyevna! (*She looks round at him.*) I will just pay my respects to you and then leave you at once (*kisses her hand warmly*). I was told to wait until morning, but I hadn't the patience to wait any longer. . . .

(LYUBOV ANDREYEVNA *looks at him in perplexity.*)

VARYA (*through her tears*). This is Petya Trofimov.

TROFIMOV. Petya Trofimov, who was your Grisha's tutor. . . . Can I have changed so much?

(LYUBOV ANDREYEVNA *embraces him and weeps quietly.*)

GAEV (*in confusion*). There, there, Lyuba.

VARYA (*crying*). I told you, Petya, to wait till to-morrow.

LYUBOV. My Grisha . . . my boy . . . Grisha . . . my son!

VARYA. We can't help it, mamma, it is God's will.

TROFIMOV (*softly through his tears*). There . . . there.

LYUBOV (*weeping quietly*). My boy was lost . . . drowned. Why? Oh, why, dear Petya? (*More quietly*) Anya is asleep in there, and I'm talking loudly . . . making this noise. . . . But, Petya? Why have you grown so ugly? Why do you look so old?

TROFIMOV. A peasant-woman in the train called me a mangy-looking gentleman.

LYUBOV. You were quite a boy then, a pretty little student, and now your hair's thin—and spectacles. Are you really a student still? (*goes towards the door*).

TROFIMOV. I seem likely to be a perpetual student.

LYUBOV (*kisses her brother, then* VARYA). Well, go to bed. . . . You are older too, Leonid.

PISHTCHIK (*follows her*). I suppose it's time we were asleep. . . . Ugh! my gout. I'm staying the night; Lyubov Andreyevna, my dear soul, if you could . . . to-morrow morning . . . 240 roubles.

GAEV. That's always his story.

PISHTCHIK. 240 roubles . . . to pay the interest on my mortgage.

LYUBOV. My dear man, I have no money.

PISHTCHIK. I'll pay it back, my dear . . . a trifling sum.

LYUBOV. Oh, well, Leonid will give it you. . . . You give him the money, Leonid.

GAEV. Me give it him! Let him wait till he gets it!

LYUBOV. It can't be helped, give it him. He needs it. He'll pay it back.

(LYUBOV ANDREYEVNA, TROFIMOV, PISHTCHIK *and* FIRS *go out.* GAEV, VARYA *and* YASHA *remain.*)

GAEV. Sister hasn't got out of the habit of flinging away her money. (*To* YASHA) Get away, my good fellow, you smell of the hen-house.

YASHA (*with a grin*). And you, Leonid Andreyevitch, are just the same as ever.

GAEV. What's that ? (*To* VARYA) What did he say ?

VARYA (*to* YASHA). Your mother has come from the village ; she has been sitting in the servants' room since yesterday, waiting to see you.

YASHA. Oh, bother her !

VARYA. For shame !

YASHA. What's the hurry ? She might just as well have come to-morrow (*goes out*).

VARYA. Mamma's just the same as ever, she hasn't changed a bit. If she had her own way, she'd give away everything.

GAEV. Yes (*a pause*). If a great many remedies are suggested for some disease, it means that the disease is incurable. I keep thinking and racking my brains ; I have many schemes, a great many, and that really means none. If we could only come in for a legacy from somebody, or marry our Anya to a very rich man, or we might go to Yaroslavl and try our luck with our old aunt, the Countess. She's very, very rich, you know.

VARYA (*weeps*). If God would help us.

GAEV. Don't blubber. Aunt's very rich, but she doesn't like us. First, sister married a lawyer instead of a nobleman. . . .

(ANYA *appears in the doorway.*)

GAEV. And then her conduct, one can't call it virtuous. She is good, and kind, and nice, and

I love her, but, however one allows for extenuating circumstances, there's no denying that she's an immoral woman. One feels it in her slightest gesture.

VARYA (*in a whisper*). Anya's in the doorway.

GAEV. What do you say ? (*a pause*). It's queer, there seems to be something wrong with my right eye. I don't see as well as I did. And on Thursday when I was in the district Court . . .

(*Enter* ANYA.)

VARYA. Why aren't you asleep, Anya ?

ANYA. I can't get to sleep.

GAEV. My pet (*kisses* ANYA'S *face and hands*). My child (*weeps*). You are not my niece, you are my angel, you are everything to me. Believe me, believe . . .

ANYA. I believe you, uncle. Everyone loves you and respects you . . . but, uncle dear, you must be silent . . . simply be silent. What were you saying just now about my mother, about your own sister ? What made you say that ?

GAEV. Yes, yes . . . (*puts his hand over his face*). Really, that was awful ! My God, save me ! And to-day I made a speech to the bookcase . . . so stupid ! And only when I had finished, I saw how stupid it was.

VARYA. It's true, uncle, you ought to keep quiet. Don't talk, that's all.

ANYA. If you could keep from talking, it would make things easier for you, too.

GAEV. I won't speak (*kisses* ANYA'S *and* VARYA'S *hands*). I'll be silent. Only this is about business. On Thursday I was in the district Court ; well, there was a large party of us there and we began talking of one thing and another, and this and that, and do you know, I believe that it will be possible to raise a loan on an I.O.U. to pay the arrears on the mortgage.

VARYA. If the Lord would help us!

GAEV. I'm going on Tuesday; I'll talk of it again. (*To* VARYA) Don't blubber. (*To* ANYA) Your mamma will talk to Lopahin; of course, he won't refuse her. And as soon as you're rested you shall go to Yaroslavl to the Countess, your great-aunt. So we shall all set to work in three directions at once, and the business is done. We shall pay off arrears, I'm convinced of it (*puts a caramel in his mouth*). I swear on my honour, I swear by anything you like, the estate shan't be sold (*excitedly*). By my own happiness, I swear it! Here's my hand on it, call me the basest, vilest of men, if I let it come to an auction! Upon my soul I swear it!

ANYA (*her equanimity has returned, she is quite happy*). How good you are, uncle, and how clever! (*embraces her uncle*). I'm at peace now! Quite at peace! I'm happy!

(*Enter* FIRS.)

FIRS (*reproachfully*). Leonid Andreyevitch, have you no fear of God? When are you going to bed?

GAEV. Directly, directly. You can go, Firs. I'll . . . yes, I will undress myself. Come, children, bye-bye. We'll go into details to-morrow, but now go to bed (*kisses* ANYA *and* VARYA). I'm a man of the eighties. They run down that period, but still I can say I have had to suffer not a little for my convictions in my life. It's not for nothing that the peasant loves me. One must know the peasant! One must know how . . .

ANYA. At it again, uncle!

VARYA. Uncle dear, you'd better be quiet!

FIRS (*angrily*). Leonid Andreyevitch!

GAEV. I'm coming. I'm coming. Go to bed. Potted the shot—there's a shot for you! A beauty! (*goes out*, FIRS *hobbling after him*).

ANYA. My mind's at rest now. I don't want to go to Yaroslavl, I don't like my great-aunt, but still my mind's at rest. Thanks to uncle (*sits down*).

VARYA. We must go to bed. I'm going. Something unpleasant happened while you were away. In the old servants' quarters there are only the old servants, as you know—Efimyushka, Polya and Yevstigney—and Karp too. They began letting stray people in to spend the night—I said nothing. But all at once I heard they had been spreading a report that I gave them nothing but pease pudding to eat. Out of stinginess, you know. . . . And it was all Yevstigney's doing. . . . Very well, I said to myself. . . . If that's how it is, I thought, wait a bit. I sent for Yevstigney . . . (*yawns*). He comes. . . . "How's this, Yevstigney," I said, "you could be such a fool as to? . . ." (*Looking at* ANYA) Anitchka! (*a pause*). She's asleep (*puts her arm round* ANYA). Come to bed . . . come along! (*leads her*). My darling has fallen asleep! Come . . . (*They go.*)

(*Far away beyond the orchard a shepherd plays

on a pipe. TROFIMOV *crosses the stage and, seeing* VARYA *and* ANYA, *stands still.*)

VARYA. 'Sh! She's asleep, asleep. Come, my own.

ANYA (*softly, half asleep*). I'm so tired. Still those bells. Uncle . . . dear . . . mamma and uncle. . . .

VARYA. Come, my own, come along.

(*They go into* ANYA'S *room.*)

TROFIMOV (*tenderly*). My sunshine! My spring

CURTAIN.

ACT II

The open country. An old shrine, long abandoned and fallen out of the perpendicular; near it a well, large stones that have apparently once been tombstones, and an old garden seat. The road to GAEV'S *house is seen. On one side rise dark poplars; and there the cherry orchard begins. In the distance a row of telegraph poles and far, far away on the horizon there is faintly outlined a great town, only visible in very fine clear weather. It is near sunset.* CHARLOTTA, YASHA *and* DUNYASHA *are sitting on the seat.* EPIHODOV *is standing near, playing something mournful on a guitar. All sit plunged in thought.* CHARLOTTA *wears an old forage cap; she has taken a gun from her shoulder and is tightening the buckle on the strap.*

CHARLOTTA (*musingly*). I haven't a real passport of my own, and I don't know how old I am, and I always feel that I'm a young thing. When I was a little girl, my father and mother used to travel about to fairs and give performances—very good ones. And I used to dance *salto-mortale* and all sorts of things. And when papa and mamma died, a German lady took me and had me educated.

And so I grew up and became a governess. But where I came from, and who I am, I don't know. . . . Who my parents were, very likely they weren't married . . . I don't know (*takes a cucumber out of her pocket and eats*). I know nothing at all (*a pause*). One wants to talk and has no one to talk to . . . I have nobody.

EPIHODOV (*plays on the guitar and sings*). "What care I for the noisy world! What care I for friends or foes!" How agreeable it is to play on the mandoline!

DUNYASHA. That's a guitar, not a mandoline (*looks in a hand-mirror and powders herself*).

EPIHODOV. To a man mad with love, it's a mandoline. (*Sings*) "Were her heart but aglow with love's mutual flame." (YASHA *joins in.*)

CHARLOTTA. How shockingly these people sing! Foo! Like jackals!

DUNYASHA (*to* YASHA). What happiness, though, to visit foreign lands.

YASHA. Ah, yes! I rather agree with you there (*yawns, then lights a cigar*).

EPIHODOV. That's comprehensible. In foreign lands everything has long since reached full complexion.

YASHA. That's so, of course.

EPIHODOV. I'm a cultivated man, I read remarkable books of all sorts, but I can never make out the tendency I am myself precisely inclined for, whether to live or to shoot myself, speaking precisely, but nevertheless I always carry a revolver. Here it is . . . (*shows revolver*).

CHARLOTTA. I've had enough, and now I'm going (*puts on the gun*). Epihodov, you're a very clever fellow, and a very terrible one too, all the women must be wild about you. Br-r-r! (*goes*). These clever fellows are all so stupid; there's not a creature for me to speak to. . . . Always alone, alone, nobody belonging to me . . . and who I am, and why I'm on earth, I don't know (*walks away slowly*).

EPIHODOV. Speaking precisely, not touching upon other subjects, I'm bound to admit about myself, that destiny behaves mercilessly to me, as a storm to a little boat. If, let us suppose, I am mistaken, then why did I wake up this morning, to quote an example, and look round, and there on my chest was a spider of fearful magnitude . . . like this (*shows with both hands*). And then I take up a jug of kvass, to quench my thirst, and in it there is something in the highest degree unseemly of the nature of a cockroach (*a pause*). Have you read Buckle? (*a pause*). I am desirous of troubling you, Dunyasha, with a couple of words.

DUNYASHA. Well, speak.

EPIHODOV. I should be desirous to speak with you alone (*sighs*).

DUNYASHA (*embarrassed*). Well—only bring me my mantle first. It's by the cupboard. It's rather damp here.

EPIHODOV. Certainly. I will fetch it. Now I know what I must do with my revolver (*takes guitar and goes off playing on it*).

YASHA. Two and twenty misfortunes! Between ourselves, he's a fool (*yawns*).

DUNYASHA. God grant he doesn't shoot himself! (*a pause*). I am so nervous, I'm always in a flutter. I was a little girl when I was taken into our lady's house, and now I have quite grown out of peasant ways, and my hands are white, as white as a lady's. I'm such a delicate, sensitive creature, I'm afraid of everything. I'm so frightened. And if you deceive me, Yasha, I don't know what will become of my nerves.

YASHA (*kisses her*). You're a peach! Of course a girl must never forget herself; what I dislike more than anything is a girl being flighty in her behaviour.

DUNYASHA. I'm passionately in love with you, Yasha; you are a man of culture—you can give your opinion about anything (*a pause*).

YASHA (*yawns*). Yes, that's so. My opinion is this: if a girl loves anyone, that means that she has no principles (*a pause*). It's pleasant smoking a cigar in the open air (*listens*). Someone's coming this way . . . it's the gentlefolk (DUNYASHA *embraces him impulsively*). Go home, as though you had been to the river to bathe; go by that path, or else they'll meet you and suppose I have made an appointment with you here. That I can't endure.

DUNYASHA (*coughing softly*). The cigar has made my head ache . . . (*goes off*).

(YASHA *remains sitting near the shrine. Enter* LYUBOV ANDREYEVNA, GAEV *and* LOPAHIN.)

LOPAHIN. You must make up your mind once for all—there's no time to lose. It's quite a simple question, you know. Will you consent to letting the land for building or not? One word in answer: Yes or no? Only one word!

LYUBOV. Who is smoking such horrible cigars here? (*sits down*).

GAEV. Now the railway line has been brought near, it's made things very convenient (*sits down*). Here we have been over and lunched in town. Cannon off the white! I should like to go home and have a game.

LYUBOV. You have plenty of time.

LOPAHIN. Only one word! (*Beseechingly*) Give me an answer!

GAEV (*yawning*). What do you say?

LYUBOV (*looks in her purse*). I had quite a lot of money here yesterday, and there's scarcely any left to-day. My poor Varya feeds us all on milk soup for the sake of economy; the old folks in the kitchen get nothing but pease pudding, while I waste my money in a senseless way (*drops purse, scattering gold pieces*). There, they have all fallen out! (*annoyed*).

YASHA. Allow me, I'll soon pick them up (*collects the coins*).

LYUBOV. Pray do, Yasha. And what did I go off to the town to lunch for? Your restaurant's a wretched place with its music and the tablecloth smelling of soap. . . . Why drink so much, Leonid? And eat so much? And talk so much? To-day you talked a great deal again in the restaurant, and all so inappropriately. About the era of the 'seventies, about the decadents. And to whom? Talking to waiters about decadents!

LOPAHIN. Yes.

GAEV (*waving his hand*). I'm incorrigible; that's evident. (*Irritably to* YASHA) Why is it you keep fidgeting about in front of us!

YASHA (*laughs*). I can't help laughing when I hear your voice.

GAEV (*to his sister*). Either I or he . . .

LYUBOV. Get along! Go away, Yasha.

YASHA (*gives* LYUBOV ANDREYEVNA *her purse*). Directly (*hardly able to suppress his laughter*). This minute . . . (*goes off*).

LOPAHIN. Deriganov, the millionaire, means to buy your estate. They say he is coming to the sale himself.

LYUBOV. Where did you hear that?

LOPAHIN. That's what they say in town.

GAEV. Our aunt in Yaroslavl has promised to send help; but when, and how much she will send, we don't know.

LOPAHIN. How much will she send? A hundred thousand? Two hundred?

LYUBOV. Oh, well! . . . Ten or fifteen thousand, and we must be thankful to get that.

LOPAHIN. Forgive me, but such reckless people as you are—such queer, unbusiness-like people—I never met in my life. One tells you in plain Russian your estate is going to be sold, and you seem not to understand it.

LYUBOV. What are we to do? Tell us what to do.

LOPAHIN. I do tell you every day. Every day I say the same thing. You absolutely must let the cherry orchard and the land on building leases; and do it at once, as quick as may be—the auction's close upon us ! Do understand ! Once make up your mind to build villas, and you can raise as much money as you like, and then you are saved.

LYUBOV. Villas and summer visitors—forgive me saying so—it's so vulgar.

GAEV. There I perfectly agree with you.

LOPAHIN. I shall sob, or scream, or fall into a fit. I can't stand it ! You drive me mad ! (*To* GAEV) You're an old woman !

GAEV. What do you say ?

LOPAHIN. An old woman ! (*gets up to go*).

LYUBOV (*in dismay*). No, don't go ! Do stay, my dear friend ! Perhaps we shall think of something.

LOPAHIN. What is there to think of ?

LYUBOV. Don't go, I entreat you ! With you here it's more cheerful, anyway (*a pause*). I keep expecting something, as though the house were going to fall about our ears.

GAEV (*in profound dejection*). Potted the white ! It fails—a kiss.

LYUBOV. We have been great sinners. . . .

LOPAHIN. You have no sins to repent of.

GAEV (*puts a caramel in his mouth*). They say I've eaten up my property in caramels (*laughs*).

LYUBOV. Oh, my sins ! I've always thrown my money away recklessly like a lunatic. I married a man who made nothing but debts. My husband died of champagne—he drank dreadfully. To my misery I loved another man, and immediately—it was my first punishment—the blow fell upon me, here, in the river . . . my boy was drowned and I went abroad—went away for ever, never to return, not to see that river again . . . I shut my eyes, and fled, distracted, and *he* after me . . . pitilessly, brutally. I bought a villa at Mentone, for *he* fell ill there, and for three years I had no rest day or night. His illness wore me out, my soul was dried up. And last year, when my villa was sold to pay my debts, I went to Paris and there he robbed me of everything and abandoned me for another woman; and I tried to poison myself. . . . So stupid, so shameful! . . . And suddenly I felt a yearning for Russia, for my country, for my little girl . . . (*dries her tears*). Lord, Lord, be merciful! Forgive my sins! Do not chastise me more! (*Takes a telegram out of her pocket*) I got this to-day from Paris. He implores forgiveness, entreats me to return (*tears up the telegram*). I fancy there is music somewhere (*listens*).

GAEV. That's our famous Jewish orchestra. You remember, four violins, a flute and a double bass.

LYUBOV. That still in existence? We ought to send for them one evening, and give a dance.

LOPAHIN (*listens*). I can't hear. . . . (*Hums softly*) "For money the Germans will turn a Russian into a Frenchman." (*Laughs*) I did see such a piece at the theatre yesterday! It was funny!

LYUBOV. And most likely there was nothing funny in it. You shouldn't look at plays, you should look at yourselves a little oftener. How grey your lives are! How much nonsense you talk.

LOPAHIN. That's true. One may say honestly, we live a fool's life (*pause*). My father was a peasant, an idiot; he knew nothing and taught me nothing, only beat me when he was drunk, and always with his stick. In reality I am just such another blockhead and idiot. I've learnt nothing properly. I write a wretched hand. I write so that I feel ashamed before folks, like a pig.

LYUBOV. You ought to get married, my dear fellow.

LOPAHIN. Yes . . . that's true.

LYUBOV. You should marry our Varya, she's a good girl.

LOPAHIN. Yes.

LYUBOV. She's a good-natured girl, she's busy all day long, and what's more, she loves you. And you have liked her for ever so long.

LOPAHIN. Well? I'm not against it. . . . She's a good girl (*pause*).

GAEV. I've been offered a place in the bank: 6,000 roubles a year. Did you know?

LYUBOV. You would never do for that! You must stay as you are.

(*Enter* FIRS *with overcoat.*)

FIRS. Put it on, sir, it's damp.

GAEV (*putting it on*). You bother me, old fellow.

FIRS. You can't go on like this. You went away in the morning without leaving word (*looks him over*).

LYUBOV. You look older, Firs!

FIRS. What is your pleasure?

LOPAHIN. You look older, she said.

FIRS. I've had a long life. They were arranging

my wedding before your papa was born . . . (*laughs*). I was the head footman before the emancipation came. I wouldn't consent to be set free then; I stayed on with the old master . . . (*a pause*). I remember what rejoicings they made and didn't know themselves what they were rejoicing over.

LOPAHIN. Those were fine old times. There was flogging anyway.

FIRS (*not hearing*). To be sure! The peasants knew their place, and the masters knew theirs; but now they're all at sixes and sevens, there's no making it out.

GAEV. Hold your tongue, Firs. I must go to town to-morrow. I have been promised an introduction to a general, who might let us have a loan.

LOPAHIN. You won't bring that off. And you won't pay your arrears, you may rest assured of that.

LYUBOV. That's all his nonsense. There is no such general.

(*Enter* TROFIMOV, ANYA *and* VARYA.)

GAEV. Here come our girls.

ANYA. There's mamma on the seat.

LYUBOV (*tenderly*). Come here, come along. My darlings! (*embraces* ANYA *and* VARYA). If you only knew how I love you both. Sit beside me, there, like that. (*All sit down.*)

LOPAHIN. Our perpetual student is always with the young ladies.

TROFIMOV. That's not your business.

LOPAHIN. He'll soon be fifty, and he's still a student.

TROFIMOV. Drop your idiotic jokes.

LOPAHIN. Why are you so cross, you queer fish?

TROFIMOV. Oh, don't persist!

LOPAHIN (*laughs*). Allow me to ask you what's your idea of me?

TROFIMOV. I'll tell you my idea of you, Yermolay Alexeyevitch: you are a rich man, you'll soon be a millionaire. Well, just as in the economy of nature a wild beast is of use, who devours everything that comes in his way, so you too have your use.

(*All laugh.*)

VARYA. Better tell us something about the planets, Petya.

LYUBOV. No, let us go on with the conversation we had yesterday.

TROFIMOV. What was it about?

GAEV. About pride.

TROFIMOV. We had a long conversation yesterday, but we came to no conclusion. In pride, in your sense of it, there is something mystical. Perhaps you are right from your point of view; but if one looks at it simply, without subtlety, what sort of pride can there be, what sense is there in it, if man in his physiological formation is very imperfect, if in the immense majority of cases he is coarse, dull-witted, profoundly unhappy? One must give up glorification of self. One should work, and nothing else.

GAEV. One must die in any case.

TROFIMOV. Who knows? And what does it mean—dying? Perhaps man has a hundred senses, and only the five we know are lost at death, while the other ninety-five remain alive.

LYUBOV. How clever you are, Petya!

LOPAHIN (*ironically*). Fearfully clever!

TROFIMOV. Humanity progresses, perfecting its powers. Everything that is beyond its ken now will one day become familiar and comprehensible; only we must work, we must with all our powers aid the seeker after truth. Here among us in Russia the workers are few in number as yet. The vast majority of the intellectual people I know, seek nothing, do nothing, are not fit as yet for work of any kind. They call themselves intellectual, but they treat their servants as inferiors, behave to the peasants as though they were animals, learn little, read nothing seriously, do practically nothing, only talk about science and know very little about art. They are all serious people, they all have severe faces, they all talk of weighty matters and air their theories, and yet the vast majority of us—ninety-nine per cent.—live like savages, at the least thing fly to blows and abuse, eat piggishly, sleep in filth and stuffiness, bugs everywhere, stench and damp and moral impurity. And it's clear all our fine talk is only to divert our attention and other people's. Show me where to find the crèches there's so much talk about, and the reading-rooms? They only exist in novels: in real life there are none of them. There is nothing but filth and vulgarity and Asiatic apathy. I fear and dislike very serious faces. I'm afraid of serious conversations. We should do better to be silent.

LOPAHIN. You know, I get up at five o'clock in the morning, and I work from morning to night;

and I've money, my own and other people's, always passing through my hands, and I see what people are made of all round me. One has only to begin to do anything to see how few honest, decent people there are. Sometimes when I lie awake at night, I think: "Oh! Lord, thou hast given us immense forests, boundless plains, the widest horizons, and living here we ourselves ought really to be giants."

LYUBOV. You ask for giants! They are no good except in story-books; in real life they frighten us.

(EPIHODOV *advances in the background, playing on the guitar.*)

LYUBOV (*dreamily*). There goes Epihodov.

ANYA (*dreamily*). There goes Epihodov.

GAEV. The sun has set, my friends.

TROFIMOV. Yes.

GAEV (*not loudly, but, as it were, declaiming*). O nature, divine nature, thou art bright with eternal lustre, beautiful and indifferent! Thou, whom we call mother, thou dost unite within thee life and death! Thou dost give life and dost destroy!

VARYA (*in a tone of supplication*). Uncle!

ANYA. Uncle, you are at it again!

TROFIMOV. You'd much better be cannoning off the red!

GAEV. I'll hold my tongue, I will.

(*All sit plunged in thought. Perfect stillness. The only thing audible is the muttering of* FIRS. *Suddenly there is a sound in the distance, as it were from the sky—the sound of a breaking harp-string, mournfully dying away.*)

LYUBOV. What is that?

LOPAHIN. I don't know. Somewhere far away a bucket fallen and broken in the pits. But somewhere very far away.

GAEV. It might be a bird of some sort—such as a heron.

TROFIMOV. Or an owl.

LYUBOV (*shudders*). I don't know why, but it's horrid (*a pause*).

FIRS. It was the same before the calamity—the owl hooted and the samovar hissed all the time.

GAEV. Before what calamity?

FIRS. Before the emancipation (*a pause*).

LYUBOV. Come, my friends, let us be going; evening is falling. (*To* ANYA) There are tears in your eyes. What is it, darling? (*embraces her*).

ANYA. Nothing, mamma; it's nothing.

TROFIMOV. There is somebody coming.

(*The wayfarer appears in a shabby white forage cap and an overcoat; he is slightly drunk.*)

WAYFARER. Allow me to inquire, can I get to the station this way?

GAEV. Yes. Go along that road.

WAYFARER. I thank you most feelingly (*coughing*). The weather is superb. (*Declaims*) My brother, my suffering brother! . . . Come out to the Volga! Whose groan do you hear? . . . (*To* VARYA) Mademoiselle, vouchsafe a hungry Russian thirty kopecks.

(VARYA *utters a shriek of alarm.*)

LOPAHIN (*angrily*). There's a right and a wrong way of doing everything!

LYUBOV (*hurriedly*). Here, take this (*looks in her purse*). I've no silver. No matter—here's gold for you.

WAYFARER. I thank you most feelingly! (*goes off*). (*Laughter.*)

VARYA (*frightened*). I'm going home—I'm going . . . Oh, mamma, the servants have nothing to eat, and you gave him gold!

LYUBOV. There's no doing anything with me. I'm so silly! When we get home, I'll give you all I possess. Yermolay Alexeyevitch, you will lend me some more . . .!

LOPAHIN. I will.

LYUBOV. Come, friends, it's time to be going. And Varya, we have made a match of it for you. I congratulate you.

VARYA (*through her tears*). Mamma, that's not a joking matter.

LOPAHIN. "Ophelia, get thee to a nunnery!"

GAEV. My hands are trembling; it's a long while since I had a game of billiards.

LOPAHIN. "Ophelia! Nymph, in thy orisons be all my sins remember'd."

LYUBOV. Come, it will soon be supper-time.

VARYA. How he frightened me! My heart's simply throbbing.

LOPAHIN. Let me remind you, ladies and gentlemen: on the 22nd of August the cherry orchard will be sold. Think about that! Think about it!

(*All go off, except* TROFIMOV *and* ANYA.)

ANYA (*laughing*). I'm grateful to the wayfarer! He frightened Varya and we are left alone.

TROFIMOV. Varya's afraid we shall fall in love

with each other, and for days together she won't leave us. With her narrow brain she can't grasp that we are above love. To eliminate the petty and transitory which hinders us from being free and happy—that is the aim and meaning of our life. Forward! We go forward irresistibly towards the bright star that shines yonder in the distance. Forward! Do not lag behind, friends.

ANYA (*claps her hands*). How well you speak! (*a pause*). It is divine here to-day.

TROFIMOV. Yes, it's glorious weather.

ANYA. Somehow, Petya, you've made me so that I don't love the cherry orchard as I used to. I used to love it so dearly. I used to think that there was no spot on earth like our garden.

TROFIMOV. All Russia is our garden. The earth is great and beautiful—there are many beautiful places in it (*a pause*). Think only, Anya, your grandfather, and great-grandfather, and all your ancestors were slave-owners—the owners of living souls—and from every cherry in the orchard, from every leaf, from every trunk there are human creatures looking at you. Cannot you hear their voices? Oh, it is awful! Your orchard is a fearful thing, and when in the evening or at night one walks about the orchard, the old bark on the trees glimmers dimly in the dusk, and the old cherry trees seem to be dreaming of centuries gone by and tortured by fearful visions. Yes! We are at least two hundred years behind, we have really gained nothing yet, we have no definite attitude to the past, we do nothing but theorise or complain of depression or drink vodka. It is clear that to begin to live in the present we must first expiate our past, we must break with it; and we can expiate it only by suffering, by extraordinary unceasing labour. Understand that, Anya.

ANYA. The house we live in has long ceased to be our own, and I shall leave it, I give you my word.

TROFIMOV. If you have the house keys, fling them into the well and go away. Be free as the wind.

ANYA (*in ecstasy*). How beautifully you said that!

TROFIMOV. Believe me, Anya, believe me! I am not thirty yet, I am young, I am still a student, but I have gone through so much already! As soon as winter comes I am hungry, sick, careworn, poor as a beggar, and what ups and downs of fortune have I not known! And my soul was always, every minute, day and night, full of inexplicable forebodings. I have a foreboding of happiness, Anya. I see glimpses of it already.

ANYA (*pensively*). The moon is rising.

(EPIHODOV *is heard playing still the same mournful song on the guitar. The moon rises. Somewhere near the poplars* VARYA *is looking for* ANYA *and calling* "Anya! where are you?")

TROFIMOV. Yes, the moon is rising (*a pause*). Here is happiness—here it comes! It is coming nearer and nearer; already I can hear its footsteps. And if we never see it—if we may never know it—what does it matter? Others will see it after us.

VARYA'S VOICE. Anya! Where are you?

TROFIMOV. That Varya again! (*Angrily*) It's revolting!

ANYA. Well, let's go down to the river. It's lovely there.

TROFIMOV. Yes, let's go. (*They go.*)

VARYA'S VOICE. Anya! Anya!

CURTAIN.

ACT III

A drawing-room divided by an arch from a larger drawing-room. A chandelier burning. The Jewish orchestra, the same that was mentioned in Act II, is heard playing in the ante-room. It is evening. In the larger drawing-room they are dancing the grand chain. The voice of SEMYONOV-PISHTCHIK: "Promenade à une paire!" *Then enter the drawing-room in couples, first* PISHTCHIK *and* CHARLOTTA IVANOVNA, *then* TROFIMOV *and* LYUBOV ANDREYEVNA, *thirdly* ANYA *with the Post-Office Clerk, fourthly* VARYA *with the Station Master, and other guests.* VARYA *is quietly weeping and wiping away her tears as she dances. In the last couple is* DUNYASHA. *They move across the drawing-room.* PISHTCHIK *shouts:* "Grand rond, balancez!" *and* "Les Cavaliers à genou et remerciez vos dames."

FIRS *in a swallow-tail coat brings in seltzer water on a tray.* PISHTCHIK *and* TROFIMOV *enter the drawing-room.*

PISHTCHIK. I am a full-blooded man; I have already had two strokes. Dancing's hard work for me, but as they say, if you're in the pack, you must bark with the rest. I'm as strong, I may say, as a horse. My parent, who would have his joke—may the Kingdom of Heaven be his!—used to say about our origin that the ancient stock of the Semyonov-Pishtchiks was derived from the very horse that Caligula made a member of the senate (*sits down*). But I've no money, that's where the mischief is. A hungry dog believes in nothing but meat . . . (*snores, but at once wakes up*). That's like me . . . I can think of nothing but money.

TROFIMOV. There really is something horsy about your appearance.

PISHTCHIK. Well . . . a horse is a fine beast . . . a horse can be sold.

(*There is the sound of billiards being played in an adjoining room.* VARYA *appears in the arch leading to the larger drawing-room.*)

TROFIMOV (*teasing*). Madame Lopahin! Madame Lopahin!

VARYA (*angrily*). Mangy-looking gentleman!

TROFIMOV. Yes, I am a mangy-looking gentleman, and I'm proud of it!

VARYA (*pondering bitterly*). Here we have hired musicians and nothing to pay them! (*goes out*).

TROFIMOV (*to* PISHTCHIK). If the energy you have wasted during your lifetime in trying to find the money to pay your interest, had gone to something else, you might in the end have turned the world upside down.

PISHTCHIK. Nietzsche, the philosopher, a very great and celebrated man . . . of enormous intellect . . . says in his works, that one can make forged bank-notes.

TROFIMOV. Why, have you read Nietzsche?

PISHTCHIK. What next . . . Dashenka told me. . . . And now I am in such a position, I might just as well forge bank-notes. The day after to-morrow I must pay 310 roubles—130 I have procured (*feels in his pockets, in alarm*). The money's gone! I have lost my money! (*Through his tears*) Where's the money? (*Gleefully*) Why here it is behind the lining. . . . It has made me hot all over.

(*Enter* LYUBOV ANDREYEVNA *and* CHARLOTTA IVANOVNA.)

LYUBOV (*hums the Lezginka*). Why is Leonid so long? What can he be doing in town? (*To* DUNYASHA) Offer the musicians some tea.

TROFIMOV. The sale hasn't taken place, most likely.

LYUBOV. It's the wrong time to have the orchestra, and the wrong time to give a dance. Well, never mind (*sits down and hums softly*).

CHARLOTTA (*gives* PISHTCHIK *a pack of cards*). Here's a pack of cards. Think of any card you like.

PISHTCHIK. I've thought of one.

CHARLOTTA. Shuffle the pack now. That's right. Give it here, my dear Mr. Pishtchik. Ein, zwei, drei—now look, it's in your breast pocket.

PISHTCHIK (*taking a card out of his breast pocket*). The eight of spades! Perfectly right! (*Wonderingly*) Fancy that now!

CHARLOTTA (*holding pack of cards in her hands, to* TROFIMOV). Tell me quickly which is the top card.

TROFIMOV. Well, the queen of spades.

CHARLOTTA. It is! (*To* PISHTCHIK) Well, which card is uppermost?

PISHTCHIK. The ace of hearts.

CHARLOTTA. It is! (*claps her hands, pack of cards disappears*). Ah! what lovely weather it is to-day!

(*A mysterious feminine voice which seems coming out of the floor answers her.* "Oh, yes, it's magnificent weather, madam.")

CHARLOTTA. You are my perfect ideal.

VOICE. And I greatly admire you too, madam.

STATION MASTER (*applauding*). The lady ventriloquist—bravo!

PISHTCHIK (*wonderingly*). Fancy that now! Most enchanting Charlotta Ivanovna. I'm simply in love with you.

CHARLOTTA. In love? (*shrugging shoulders*). What do you know of love, guter Mensch, aber schlechter Musikant.

TROFIMOV (*pats* PISHTCHIK *on the shoulder*). You dear old horse. . . .

CHARLOTTA. Attention, please! Another trick! (*takes a travelling rug from a chair*). Here's a very good rug; I want to sell it (*shaking it out*). Doesn't anyone want to buy it?

PISHTCHIK (*wonderingly*). Fancy that!

CHARLOTTA. Ein, zwei, drei! (*quickly picks up rug she has dropped; behind the rug stands* ANYA; *she makes a curtsey, runs to her mother, embraces her and runs back into the larger drawing-room amidst general enthusiasm.*)

LYUBOV (*applauds*). Bravo! Bravo!

CHARLOTTA. Now again! Ein, zwei, drei! (*lifts*

up the rug ; behind the rug stands VARYA, *bowing*).

PISHTCHIK (*wonderingly*). Fancy that now!

CHARLOTTA. That's the end (*throws the rug at* PISHTCHIK, *makes a curtsey, runs into the larger drawing-room*).

PISHTCHIK (*hurries after her*). Mischievous creature! Fancy! (*goes out*).

LYUBOV. And still Leonid doesn't come. I can't understand what he's doing in the town so long! Why, everything must be over by now. The estate is sold, or the sale has not taken place. Why keep us so long in suspense?

VARYA (*trying to console her*). Uncle's bought it. I feel sure of that.

TROFIMOV (*ironically*). Oh, yes!

VARYA. Great-aunt sent him an authorisation to buy it in her name, and transfer the debt. She's doing it for Anya's sake, and I'm sure God will be merciful. Uncle will buy it.

LYUBOV. My aunt in Yaroslavl sent fifteen thousand to buy the estate in her name, she doesn't trust us—but that's not enough even to pay the arrears (*hides her face in her hands*). My fate is being sealed to-day, my fate . . .

TROFIMOV (*teasing* VARYA). Madame Lopahin.

VARYA (*angrily*). Perpetual student! Twice already you've been sent down from the University.

LYUBOV. Why are you angry, Varya? He's teasing you about Lopahin. Well, what of that? Marry Lopahin if you like, he's a good man, and interesting; if you don't want to, don't! Nobody compels you, darling.

VARYA. I must tell you plainly, mamma, I look at the matter seriously; he's a good man, I like him.

LYUBOV. Well, marry him. I can't see what you're waiting for.

VARYA. Mamma, I can't make him an offer myself. For the last two years, everyone's been talking to me about him. Everyone talks; but he says nothing or else makes a joke. I see what it means. He's growing rich, he's absorbed in business, he has no thoughts for me. If I had money, were it ever so little, if I had only a hundred roubles, I'd throw everything up and go far away. I would go into a nunnery.

TROFIMOV. What bliss!

VARYA (*to* TROFIMOV). A student ought to have sense! (*In a soft tone with tears*) How ugly you've grown, Petya! How old you look! (*To* LYUBOV ANDREYEVNA, *no longer crying*) But I can't do without work, mamma; I must have something to do every minute.

(*Enter* YASHA.)

YASHA (*hardly restraining his laughter*). Epihodov has broken a billiard cue! (*goes out*).

VARYA. What is Epihodov doing here? Who gave him leave to play billiards? I can't make these people out (*goes out*).

LYUBOV. Don't tease her, Petya. You see she has grief enough without that.

TROFIMOV. She is so very officious, meddling in what's not her business. All the summer she's given Anya and me no peace. She's afraid of a love affair between us. What's it to do with her?

Besides, I have given no grounds for it. Such triviality is not in my line. We are above love!

LYUBOV. And I suppose I am beneath love. (*Very uneasily*) Why is it Leonid's not here? If only I could know whether the estate is sold or not! It seems such an incredible calamity that I really don't know what to think. I am distracted . . . I shall scream in a minute . . . . I shall do something stupid. Save me, Petya, tell me something, talk to me!

TROFIMOV. What does it matter whether the estate is sold to-day or not? That's all done with long ago. There's no turning back, the path is overgrown. Don't worry yourself, dear Lyubov Andreyevna. You mustn't deceive yourself; for once in your life you must face the truth!

LYUBOV. What truth? You see where the truth lies, but I seem to have lost my sight, I see nothing. You settle every great problem so boldly, but tell me, my dear boy, isn't it because you're young—because you haven't yet understood one of your problems through suffering? You look forward boldly, and isn't it that you don't see and don't expect anything dreadful because life is still hidden from your young eyes? You're bolder, more honest, deeper than we are, but think, be just a little magnanimous, have pity on me. I was born here, you know, my father and mother lived here, my grandfather lived here, I love this house. I can't conceive of life without the cherry orchard, and if it really must be sold, then sell me with the orchard (*embraces* TROFIMOV, *kisses him on the forehead*).

My boy was drowned here (*weeps*). Pity me, my dear kind fellow.

TROFIMOV. You know I feel for you with all my heart.

LYUBOV. But that should have been said differently, so differently (*takes out her handkerchief, telegram falls on the floor*). My heart is so heavy to-day. It's so noisy here, my soul is quivering at every sound, I'm shuddering all over, but I can't go away; I'm afraid to be quiet and alone. Don't be hard on me, Petya . . . I love you as though you were one of ourselves. I would gladly let you marry Anya—I swear I would—only, my dear boy, you must take your degree, you do nothing—you're simply tossed by fate from place to place. That's so strange. It is, isn't it? And you must do something with your beard to make it grow somehow (*laughs*). You look so funny!

TROFIMOV (*picks up the telegram*). I've no wish to be a beauty.

LYUBOV. That's a telegram from Paris. I get one every day. One yesterday and one to-day. That savage creature is ill again, he's in trouble again. He begs forgiveness, beseeches me to go, and really I ought to go to Paris to see him. You look shocked, Petya. What am I to do, my dear boy, what am I to do? He is ill, he is alone and unhappy, and who'll look after him, who'll keep him from doing the wrong thing, who'll give him his medicine at the right time? And why hide it or be silent? I love him, that's clear. I love him! I love him! He's a millstone about my neck, I'm going to the bottom with him, but I love that stone and can't live without it (*presses* TROFIMOV'S *hand*). Don't think ill of me, Petya, don't tell me anything, don't tell me . . .

TROFIMOV (*through his tears*). For God's sake forgive my frankness: why, he robbed you!

LYUBOV. No! No! No! You mustn't speak like that (*covers her ears*).

TROFIMOV. He is a wretch! You're the only person that doesn't know it! He's a worthless creature! A despicable wretch!

LYUBOV (*getting angry, but speaking with restraint*). You're twenty-six or twenty-seven years old, but you're still a schoolboy.

TROFIMOV. Possibly.

LYUBOV. You should be a man at your age! You should understand what love means! And you ought to be in love yourself. You ought to fall in love! (*angrily*). Yes, yes, and it's not purity in you, you're simply a prude, a comic fool, a freak.

TROFIMOV (*in horror*). The things she's saying!

LYUBOV. I am above love! You're not above love, but simply as our Firs here says, "You are a good-for-nothing." At your age not to have a mistress!

TROFIMOV (*in horror*). This is awful! The things she is saying! (*goes rapidly into the larger drawing-room clutching his head*). This is awful! I can't stand it! I'm going! (*goes off, but at once returns*). All is over between us! (*goes off into the ante-room*).

LYUBOV (*shouts after him*). Petya! Wait a

minute! You funny creature! I was joking! Petya! (*There is a sound of somebody running quickly downstairs and suddenly falling with a crash.* ANYA *and* VARYA *scream, but there is a sound of laughter at once*).

LYUBOV. What has happened?

(ANYA *runs in.*)

ANYA (*laughing*). Petya's fallen downstairs! (*runs out*).

LYUBOV. What a queer fellow that Petya is!

(*The Station Master stands in the middle of the larger room and reads "The Magdalene," by Alexey Tolstoy. They listen to him, but before he has recited many lines strains of a waltz are heard from the ante-room and the reading is broken off. All dance.* TROFIMOV, ANYA, VARYA *and* LYUBOV ANDREYEVNA *come in from the ante-room.*)

LYUBOV. Come, Petya—come, pure heart! I beg your pardon. Let's have a dance! (*dances with* PETYA).

(ANYA *and* VARYA *dance.* FIRS *comes in, puts his stick down near the side door.* YASHA *also comes into the drawing-room and looks on at the dancing.*)

YASHA. What is it, old man?

FIRS. I don't feel well. In old days we used to have generals, barons and admirals dancing at our balls, and now we send for the post-office clerk and the station master and even they're not over anxious to come. I am getting feeble. The old master, the grandfather, used to give sealing-wax for all complaints. I have been taking sealing-wax for twenty years or more. Perhaps that's what's kept me alive.

YASHA. You bore me, old man! (*yawns*). It's time you were done with.

FIRS. Ach, you're a good-for-nothing! (*mutters*).

(TROFIMOV *and* LYUBOV ANDREYEVNA *dance in larger room and then on to the stage*).

LYUBOV. Merci. I'll sit down a little (*sits down*). I'm tired.

(*Enter* ANYA.)

ANYA (*excitedly*). There's a man in the kitchen has been saying that the cherry orchard's been sold to-day.

LYUBOV. Sold to whom?

ANYA. He didn't say to whom. He's gone away.

(*She dances with* TROFIMOV, *and they go off into the larger room.*)

YASHA. There was an old man gossiping there, a stranger.

FIRS. Leonid Andreyevitch isn't here yet, he hasn't come back. He has his light overcoat on, *demi-saison*, he'll catch cold for sure. Ach! Foolish young things!!

LYUBOV. I feel as though I should die. Go, Yasha, find out to whom it has been sold.

YASHA. But he went away long ago, the old chap (*laughs*).

LYUBOV (*with slight vexation*). What are you laughing at? What are you pleased at?

YASHA. Epihodov is so funny. He's a silly fellow, two and twenty misfortunes.

LYUBOV. Firs, if the estate is sold, where will you go?

Firs. Where you bid me, there I'll go.

Lyubov. Why do you look like that? Are you ill? You ought to be in bed.

Firs. Yes (*ironically*). Me go to bed and who's to wait here? Who's to see to things without me? I'm the only one in all the house.

Yasha (*to* Lyubov Andreyevna). Lyubov Andreyevna, permit me to make a request of you; if you go back to Paris again, be so kind as to take me with you. It's positively impossible for me to stay here (*looking about him; in an undertone*) There's no need to say it, you see for yourself— an uncivilised country, the people have no morals, and then the dullness! The food in the kitchen's abominable, and then Firs runs after one muttering all sorts of unsuitable words. Take me with you, please do!

(*Enter* Pishtchik.)

Pishtchik. Allow me to ask you for a waltz, my dear lady. (Lyubov Andreyevna *goes with him.*) Enchanting lady, I really must borrow of you just 180 roubles (*dances*), only 180 roubles. (*They pass into the larger room.*)

Yasha (*hums softly*), "Knowest thou my soul's emotion."

(*In the larger drawing-room, a figure in a grey top hat and in check trousers is gesticulating and jumping about. Shouts of* " Bravo, Charlotta Ivanovna.")

Dunyasha (*she has stopped to powder herself*). My young lady tells me to dance. There are plenty of gentlemen, and too few ladies, but dancing makes me giddy and makes my heart beat. Firs, the post-office clerk said something to me just now that quite took my breath away.

(*Music becomes more subdued.*)

FIRS. What did he say to you?

DUNYASHA. He said I was like a flower.

YASHA (*yawns*). What ignorance! (*goes out*).

DUNYASHA. Like a flower. I am a girl of such delicate feelings, I am awfully fond of soft speeches.

FIRS. Your head's being turned.

(*Enter* EPIHODOV.)

EPIHODOV. You have no desire to see me, Dunyasha. I might be an insect (*sighs*). Ah! life!

DUNYASHA. What is it you want?

EPIHODOV. Undoubtedly you may be right (*sighs*) But of course, if one looks at it from that point of view, if I may so express myself, you have, excuse my plain speaking, reduced me to a complete state of mind. I know my destiny. Every day some misfortune befalls me and I have long ago grown accustomed to it, so that I look upon my fate with a smile. You gave me your word, and though I——

DUNYASHA. Let us have a talk later, I entreat you, but now leave me in peace, for I am lost in reverie (*plays with her fan*).

EPIHODOV. I have a misfortune every day, and if I may venture to express myself, I merely smile at it, I even laugh.

(VARYA *enters from the larger drawing-room.*)

VARYA. You still have not gone, Epihodov. What a disrespectful creature you are, really!

(*To* DUNYASHA) Go along, Dunyasha! (*To* EPIHODOV) First you play billiards and break the cue, then you go wandering about the drawing-room like a visitor!

EPIHODOV. You really cannot, if I may so express myself, call me to account like this.

VARYA. I'm not calling you to account, I'm speaking to you. You do nothing but wander from place to place and don't do your work. We keep you as a counting-house clerk, but what use you are I can't say.

EPIHODOV (*offended*). Whether I work or whether I walk, whether I eat or whether I play billiards, is a matter to be judged by persons of understanding and my elders.

VARYA. You dare to tell me that! (*Firing up*) You dare! You mean to say I've no understanding. Begone from here! This minute!

EPIHODOV (*intimidated*). I beg you to express yourself with delicacy.

VARYA (*beside herself with anger*). This moment! get out! away! (*He goes towards the door, she following him*). Two and twenty misfortunes! Take yourself off! Don't let me set eyes on you! (EPIHODOV *has gone out, behind the door his voice,* "I shall lodge a complaint against you"). What! You're coming back? (*snatches up the stick* FIRS *has put down near the door*). Come! Come! Come! I'll show you! What! you're coming? Then take that! (*she swings the stick, at the very moment that* LOPAHIN *comes in*).

LOPAHIN. Very much obliged to you!

VARYA (*angrily and ironically*). I beg your pardon!

LOPAHIN. Not at all! I humbly thank you for your kind reception!

VARYA. No need of thanks for it (*moves away, then looks round and asks softly*) I haven't hurt you?

LOPAHIN. Oh, no! Not at all! There's an immense bump coming up, though!

VOICES FROM LARGER ROOM. Lopahin has come! Yermolay Alexeyevitch!

PISHTCHIK. What do I see and hear? (*kisses* LOPAHIN). There's a whiff of cognac about you, my dear soul, and we're making merry here too!

(*Enter* LYUBOV ANDREYEVNA.)

LYUBOV. Is it you, Yermolay Alexeveyitch? Why have you been so long? Where's Leonid?

LOPAHIN. Leonid Andreyevitch arrived with me. He is coming.

LYUBOV (*in agitation*). Well! Well! Was there a sale? Speak!

LOPAHIN (*embarrassed, afraid of betraying his joy*). The sale was over at four o'clock. We missed our train—had to wait till half-past nine. (*Sighing heavily*) Ugh! I feel a little giddy.

(*Enter* GAEV. *In his right hand he has purchases, with his left hand he is wiping away his tears.*)

LYUBOV. Well, Leonid? What news? (*Impatiently, with tears*) Make haste, for God's sake!

GAEV (*makes her no answer, simply waves his hand. To* FIRS, *weeping*) Here, take them;

there's anchovies, Kertch herrings. I have eaten nothing all day. What I have been through! (*Door into the billiard room is open. There is heard a knocking of balls and the voice of* YASHA *saying "Eighty-seven."* GAEV'S *expression changes, he leaves off weeping*). I am fearfully tired. Firs, come and help me change my things (*goes to his own room across the larger drawing-room*).

PISHTCHIK. How about the sale? Tell us, do!

LYUBOV. Is the cherry orchard sold?

LOPAHIN. It is sold.

LYUBOV. Who has bought it?

LOPAHIN. I have bought it. (*A pause.* LYUBOV *is crushed; she would fall down if she were not standing near a chair and table.*)

(VARYA *takes keys from her waist-band, flings them on the floor in middle of drawing-room and goes out.*)

LOPAHIN. I have bought it! Wait a bit, ladies and gentlemen, pray. My head's a bit muddled, I can't speak (*laughs*). We came to the auction. Deriganov was there already. Leonid Andreyevitch only had 15,000 and Deriganov bid 30,000, besides the arrears, straight off. I saw how the land lay. I bid against him. I bid 40,000, he bid 45,000, I said 55, and so he went on, adding 5 thousands and I adding 10. Well . . . So it ended. I bid 90, and it was knocked down to me. Now the cherry orchard's mine! Mine! (*chuckles*). My God, the cherry orchard's mine! Tell me that I'm drunk, that I'm out of my mind, that it's all a dream (*stamps with his feet*). Don't laugh at me! If my father and my grandfather could rise from their graves and see all that has happened! How their Yermolay, ignorant, beaten Yermolay, who used to run about barefoot in winter, how that very Yermolay has bought the finest estate in the world! I have bought the estate where my father and grandfather were slaves, where they weren't even admitted into the kitchen. I am asleep, I am dreaming! It is all fancy, it is the work of your imagination plunged in the darkness of ignorance (*picks up keys, smiling fondly*). She threw away the keys; she means to show she's not the housewife now (*jingles the keys*). Well, no matter. (*The orchestra is heard tuning up.*) Hey, musicians! Play! I want to hear you. Come, all of you, and look how Yermolay Lopahin will take the axe to the cherry orchard, how the trees will fall to the ground! We will build houses on it and our grandsons and great-grandsons will see a new life springing up there. Music! Play up!

(*Music begins to play.* LYUBOV ANDREYEVNA *has sunk into a chair and is weeping bitterly.*)

LOPAHIN (*reproachfully*). Why, why didn't you listen to me? My poor friend! Dear lady, there's no turning back now. (*With tears*) Oh, if all this could be over, oh, if our miserable disjointed life could somehow soon be changed!

PISHTCHIK (*takes him by the arm, in an undertone*). She's weeping, let us go and leave her alone. Come (*takes him by the arm and leads him into the larger drawing-room*).

LOPAHIN. What's that? Musicians, play up! All must be as I wish it. (*With irony*) Here comes the new master, the owner of the cherry orchard!

(*accidentally tips over a little table, almost upsetting the candelabra*). I can pay for everything! (*goes out with* PISHTCHIK. *No one remains on the stage or in the larger drawing-room except* LYUBOV, *who sits huddled up, weeping bitterly. The music plays softly.* ANYA *and* TROFIMOV *come in quickly.* ANYA *goes up to her mother and falls on her knees before her.* TROFIMOV *stands at the entrance to the larger drawing-room*).

ANYA. Mamma! Mamma, you're crying, dear, kind, good mamma! My precious! I love you! I bless you! The cherry orchard is sold, it is gone, that's true, that's true! But don't weep, mamma! Life is still before you, you have still your good, pure heart! Let us go, let us go, darling, away from here! We will make a new garden, more splendid than this one; you will see it, you will understand. And joy, quiet, deep joy, will sink into your soul like the sun at evening! And you will smile, mamma! Come, darling, let us go!

CURTAIN.

ACT IV

SCENE: *Same as in First Act. There are neither curtains on the windows nor pictures on the walls: only a little furniture remains piled up in a corner as if for sale. There is a sense of desolation; near the outer door and in the background of the scene are packed trunks, travelling bags, etc. On the left the door is open, and from here the voices of* VARYA *and* ANYA *are audible.* LOPAHIN *is standing waiting.* YASHA *is holding a tray with glasses full of champagne. In front of the stage* EPIHODOV *is tying up a box. In the background behind the scene a hum of talk from the peasants who have come to say good-bye. The voice of* GAEV: "Thanks, brothers, thanks!"

YASHA. The peasants have come to say good-bye. In my opinion, Yermolay Alexeyevitch, the peasants are good-natured, but they don't know much about things.

(*The hum of talk dies away. Enter across front of stage* LYUBOV ANDREYEVNA *and* GAEV. *She is not weeping, but is pale; her face is quivering—she cannot speak.*)

GAEV. You gave them your purse, Lyuba. That won't do—that won't do!

LYUBOV. I couldn't help it! I couldn't help it!

(*Both go out.*)

LOPAHIN (*in the doorway, calls after them*). You will take a glass at parting? Please do. I didn't think to bring any from the town, and at the station I could only get one bottle. Please take a glass (*a pause*). What? You don't care for any? (*comes away from the door*). If I'd known, I wouldn't have bought it. Well, and I'm not going to drink it. (YASHA *carefully sets the tray down on a chair.*) You have a glass, Yasha, anyway.

YASHA. Good luck to the travellers, and luck to those that stay behind! (*drinks*). This champagne isn't the real thing, I can assure you.

LOPAHIN. It cost eight roubles the bottle (*a pause*). It's devilish cold here.

YASHA. They haven't heated the stove to-day—it's all the same since we're going (*laughs*).

LOPAHIN. What are you laughing for?

YASHA. For pleasure.

LOPAHIN. Though it's October, it's as still and sunny as though it were summer. It's just right for building! (*Looks at his watch; says in doorway*) Take note, ladies and gentlemen, the train goes in forty-seven minutes; so you ought to start for the station in twenty minutes. You must hurry up!

(TROFIMOV *comes in from out of doors wearing a greatcoat.*)

TROFIMOV. I think it must be time to start, the horses are ready. The devil only knows what's become of my goloshes; they're lost. (*In the doorway*) Anya! My goloshes aren't here. I can't find them.

LOPAHIN. And I'm getting off to Harkov. I am going in the same train with you. I'm spending all the winter at Harkov. I've been wasting all my time gossiping with you and fretting with no work to do. I can't get on without work. I don't know what to do with my hands, they flap about so queerly, as if they didn't belong to me.

TROFIMOV. Well, we're just going away, and you will take up your profitable labours again.

LOPAHIN. Do take a glass.

TROFIMOV. No, thanks.

LOPAHIN. Then you're going to Moscow now?

TROFIMOV. Yes. I shall see them as far as the town, and to-morrow I shall go on to Moscow.

LOPAHIN. Yes, I daresay, the professors aren't giving any lectures, they're waiting for your arrival.

TROFIMOV. That's not your business.

LOPAHIN. How many years have you been at the University?

TROFIMOV. Do think of something newer than that—that's stale and flat (*hunts for goloshes*). You know we shall most likely never see each other again, so let me give you one piece of advice at parting: don't wave your arms about—get out of the habit. And another thing, building villas, reckoning up that the summer visitors will in time become independent farmers—reckoning like that, that's not the thing to do either. After all, I am fond of you: you have fine delicate fingers like an artist, you've a fine delicate soul.

LOPAHIN (*embraces him*). Good-bye, my dear fellow. Thanks for everything. Let me give you money for the journey, if you need it.

TROFIMOV. What for ? I don't need it.

LOPAHIN. Why, you haven't got a halfpenny.

TROFIMOV. Yes, I have, thank you. I got some money for a translation. Here it is in my pocket, (*anxiously*) but where can my goloshes be !

VARYA (*from the next room*). Take the nasty things ! (*flings a pair of goloshes on to the stage*).

TROFIMOV. Why are you so cross, Varya ? h'm ! . . . but those aren't my goloshes.

LOPAHIN. I sowed three thousand acres with poppies in the spring, and now I have cleared forty thousand profit. And when my poppies were in flower, wasn't it a picture ! So here, as I say, I made forty thousand, and I'm offering you a loan because I can afford to. Why turn up your nose ? I am a peasant—I speak bluntly.

TROFIMOV. Your father was a peasant, mine was a chemist—and that proves absolutely nothing whatever. (LOPAHIN *takes out his pocket-book.*) Stop that—stop that. If you were to offer me two hundred thousand I wouldn't take it. I am an independent man, and everything that all of you, rich and poor alike, prize so highly and hold so dear, hasn't the slightest power over me—it's like so much fluff fluttering in the air. I can get on without you. I can pass by you. I am strong and proud. Humanity is advancing towards the highest truth, the highest happiness, which is possible on earth, and I am in the front ranks.

LOPAHIN. Will you get there ?

TROFIMOV. I shall get there (*a pause*). I shall get there, or I shall show others the way to get there.

(*In the distance is heard the stroke of an axe on a tree.*)

LOPAHIN. Good-bye, my dear fellow; it's time to be off. We turn up our noses at one another, but life is passing all the while. When I am working hard without resting, then my mind is more at ease, and it seems to me as though I too know what I exist for; but how many people there are in Russia, my dear boy, who exist, one doesn't know what for. Well, it doesn't matter. That's not what keeps things spinning. They tell me Leonid Andreyevitch has taken a situation. He is going to be a clerk at the bank—6,000 roubles a year. Only, of course, he won't stick to it—he's too lazy.

ANYA (*in the doorway*). Mamma begs you not to let them chop down the orchard until she's gone.

TROFIMOV. Yes, really, you might have the tact (*walks out across the front of the stage*).

LOPAHIN. I'll see to it! I'll see to it! Stupid fellows! (*goes out after him*).

ANYA. Has Firs been taken to the hospital?

YASHA. I told them this morning. No doubt they have taken him.

ANYA (*to* EPIHODOV, *who passes across the drawing-room*). Semyon Pantaleyevitch, inquire, please, if Firs has been taken to the hospital.

YASHA (*in a tone of offence*). I told Yegor this morning—why ask a dozen times?

EPIHODOV. Firs is advanced in years. It's my conclusive opinion no treatment would do him good; it's time he was gathered to his fathers.

And I can only envy him (*puts a trunk down on a cardboard hat-box and crushes it*). There, now, of course—I knew it would be so.

YASHA (*jeeringly*). Two and twenty misfortunes!

VARYA (*through the door*). Has Firs been taken to the hospital?

ANYA. Yes.

VARYA. Why wasn't the note for the doctor taken too?

ANYA. Oh, then, we must send it after them (*goes out*).

VARYA (*from the adjoining room*). Where's Yasha? Tell him his mother's come to say good-bye to him.

YASHA (*waves his hand*). They put me out of all patience! (DUNYASHA *has all this time been busy about the luggage. Now, when* YASHA *is left alone, she goes up to him*).

DUNYASHA. You might just give me one look, Yasha. You're going away. You're leaving me (*weeps and throws herself on his neck*).

YASHA. What are you crying for? (*drinks the champagne*). In six days I shall be in Paris again. To-morrow we shall get into the express train and roll away in a flash. I can scarcely believe it! Vive la France! It doesn't suit me here—it's not the life for me; there's no doing anything. I have seen enough of the ignorance here. I have had enough of it (*drinks champagne*). What are you crying for? Behave yourself properly, and then you won't cry.

DUNYASHA (*powders her face, looking in a pocket-

mirror). Do send me a letter from Paris. You know how I loved you, Yasha—how I loved you! I am a tender creature, Yasha.

YASHA. Here they are coming!

(*Busies himself about the trunks, humming softly. Enter* LYUBOV ANDREYEVNA, GAEV, ANYA *and* CHARLOTTA IVANOVNA.)

GAEV. We ought to be off. There's not much time now (*looking at* YASHA). What a smell of herrings!

LYUBOV. In ten minutes we must get into the carriage (*casts a look about the room*). Farewell, dear house, dear old home of our fathers! Winter will pass and spring will come, and then you will be no more; they will tear you down! How much those walls have seen! (*kisses her daughter passionately*). My treasure, how bright you look! Your eyes are sparkling like diamonds! Are you glad? Very glad?

ANYA. Very glad! A new life is beginning, mamma.

GAEV. Yes, really, everything is all right now. Before the cherry orchard was sold, we were all worried and wretched, but afterwards, when once the question was settled conclusively, irrevocably, we all felt calm and even cheerful. I am a bank clerk now—I am a financier—cannon off the red. And you, Lyuba, after all, you are looking better; there's no question of that.

LYUBOV. Yes. My nerves are better, that's true. (*Her hat and coat are handed to her*). I'm sleeping well. Carry out my things, Yasha. It's time. (*To* ANYA) My darling, we shall soon see each other again. I am going to Paris. I can live there on the money your Yaroslavl auntie sent us to buy the estate with—hurrah for auntie!—but that money won't last long.

ANYA. You'll come back soon, mamma, won't you? I'll be working up for my examination in the high school, and when I have passed that, I shall set to work and be a help to you. We will read all sorts of things together, mamma, won't we? (*kisses her mother's hands*). We will read in the autumn evenings. We'll read lots of books, and a new wonderful world will open out before us (*dreamily*). Mamma, come soon.

LYUBOV. I shall come, my precious treasure (*embraces her*).

(*Enter* LOPAHIN. CHARLOTTA *softly hums a song.*)

GAEV. Charlotta's happy; she's singing!

CHARLOTTA (*picks up a bundle like a swaddled baby*). Bye, bye, my baby. (*A baby is heard crying: "Ooah! ooah!"*). Hush, hush, my pretty boy! (*Ooah! ooah!*). Poor little thing! (*throws the bundle back*). You must please find me a situation. I can't go on like this.

LOPAHIN. We'll find you one, Charlotta Ivanovna. Don't you worry yourself.

GAEV. Everyone's leaving us. Varya's going away. We have become of no use all at once.

CHARLOTTA. There's nowhere for me to be in the town. I must go away. (*Hums*) What care I . . .

(*Enter* PISHTCHIK.)

LOPAHIN. The freak of nature!

PISHTCHIK (*gasping*). Oh! . . . let me get my breath. . . . I'm worn out . . . my most honoured . . . Give me some water.

GAEV. Want some money, I suppose? Your humble servant! I'll go out of the way of temptation (*goes out*).

PISHTCHIK. It's a long while since I have been to see you . . . dearest lady. (*To* LOPAHIN) You are here . . . glad to see you . . . a man of immense intellect . . . take . . . here (*gives* LOPAHIN *money*) 400 roubles. That leaves me owing 840.

LOPAHIN (*shrugging his shoulders in amazement*). It's like a dream. Where did you get it?

PISHTCHIK. Wait a bit . . . I'm hot . . . a most extraordinary occurrence! Some Englishmen came along and found in my land some sort of white clay. (*To* LYUBOV ANDREYEVNA) And 400 for you . . . most lovely . . . wonderful (*gives money*). The rest later (*sips water*). A young man in the train was telling me just now that a great philosopher advises jumping off a house-top. "Jump!" says he; "the whole gist of the problem lies in that." (*Wonderingly*) Fancy that, now! Water, please!

LOPAHIN. What Englishmen?

PISHTCHIK. I have made over to them the rights to dig the clay for twenty-four years . . . and now, excuse me . . . I can't stay . . . I must be trotting on. I'm going to Znoikovo . . . to Kardamanovo. . . . I'm in debt all round (*sips*). . . . To your very good health! . . . I'll come in on Thursday.

LYUBOV. We are just off to the town, and to-morrow I start for abroad.

PISHTCHIK. What! (*in agitation*). Why to the

town? Oh, I see the furniture . . . the boxes. No matter . . . (*through his tears*) . . . no matter . . . men of enormous intellect . . . these Englishmen. . . . Never mind . . . be happy. God will succour you . . . no matter . . . everything in this world must have an end (*kisses* LYUBOV ANDREYEVNA'S *hand*). If the rumour reaches you that my end has come, think of this . . . old horse, and say: "There once was such a man in the world . . . Semyonov-Pishtchik . . . the kingdom of heaven be his!" . . . most extraordinary weather . . . yes. (*Goes out in violent agitation, but at once returns and says in the doorway*) Dashenka wishes to be remembered to you (*goes out*).

LYUBOV. Now we can start. I leave with two cares in my heart. The first is leaving Firs ill. (*Looking at her watch*) We have still five minutes.

ANYA. Mamma, Firs has been taken to the hospital. Yasha sent him off this morning.

LYUBOV. My other anxiety is Varya. She is used to getting up early and working; and now, without work, she's like a fish out of water. She is thin and pale, and she's crying, poor dear! (*a pause*). You are well aware, Yermolay Alexeyevitch, I dreamed of marrying her to you, and everything seemed to show that you would get married (*whispers to* ANYA *and motions to* CHARLOTTA *and both go out*). She loves you—she suits you. And I don't know—I don't know why it is you seem, as it were, to avoid each other. I can't understand it!

LOPAHIN. I don't understand it myself, I confess. It's queer somehow, altogether. If there's still time, I'm ready now at once. Let's settle it straight off, and go ahead; but without you, I feel I shan't make her an offer.

LYUBOV. That's excellent. Why, a single moment's all that's necessary. I'll call her at once.

LOPAHIN. And there's champagne all ready too (*looking into the glasses*). Empty! Someone's emptied them already. (YASHA *coughs.*) I call that greedy.

LYUBOV (*eagerly*). Capital! We will go out. Yasha, *allez*! I'll call her in. (*At the door*) Varya, leave all that; come here. Come along! (*goes out with* YASHA).

LOPAHIN (*looking at his watch*). Yes.

(*A pause. Behind the door, smothered laughter and whispering, and, at last, enter* VARYA.)

VARYA (*looking a long while over the things*). It is strange, I can't find it anywhere.

LOPAHIN. What are you looking for?

VARYA. I packed it myself, and I can't remember (*a pause*).

LOPAHIN. Where are you going now, Varvara Mihailova?

VARYA. I? To the Ragulins. I have arranged to go to them to look after the house—as a housekeeper.

LOPAHIN. That's in Yashnovo? It'll be seventy miles away (*a pause*). So this is the end of life in this house!

VARYA (*looking among the things*). Where is it? Perhaps I put it in the trunk. Yes, life in this house is over—there will be no more of it.

LOPAHIN. And I'm just off to Harkov—by this next train. I've a lot of business there. I'm leaving Epihodov here, and I've taken him on.

VARYA. Really!

LOPAHIN. This time last year we had snow already, if you remember; but now it's so fine and sunny. Though it's cold, to be sure—three degrees of frost.

VARYA. I haven't looked (*a pause*). And besides, our thermometer's broken (*a pause*).

(*Voice at the door from the yard:* "Yermolay Alexeyevitch!")

LOPAHIN (*as though he had long been expecting this summons*). This minute!

(LOPAHIN *goes out quickly.* VARYA *sitting on the floor and laying her head on a bag full of clothes, sobs quietly. The door opens.* LYUBOV ANDREYEVNA *comes in cautiously.*)

LYUBOV. Well? (*a pause*). We must be going.

VARYA (*has wiped her eyes and is no longer crying*). Yes, mamma, it's time to start. I shall have time to get to the Ragulins to-day, if only you're not late for the train.

LYUBOV (*in the doorway*). Anya, put your things on.

(*Enter* ANYA, *then* GAEV *and* CHARLOTTA IVANOVNA. GAEV *has on a warm coat with a hood. Servants and cabmen come in.* EPIHODOV *bustles about the luggage.*)

LYUBOV. Now we can start on our travels.

ANYA (*joyfully*). On our travels!

GAEV. My friends — my dear, my precious friends! Leaving this house for ever, can I be silent? Can I refrain from giving utterance at leave-taking to those emotions which now flood all my being?

ANYA (*supplicatingly*). Uncle!

VARYA. Uncle, you mustn't!

GAEV (*dejectedly*). Cannon and into the pocket . . . I'll be quiet. . . .

(*Enter* TROFIMOV *and afterwards* LOPAHIN.)

TROFIMOV. Well, ladies and gentlemen, we must start.

LOPAHIN. Epihodov, my coat!

LYUBOV. I'll stay just one minute. It seems as though I have never seen before what the walls, what the ceilings in this house were like, and now I look at them with greediness, with such tender love.

GAEV. I remember when I was six years old sitting in that window on Trinity Day watching my father going to church.

LYUBOV. Have all the things been taken?

LOPAHIN. I think all. (*Putting on overcoat, to* EPIHODOV) You, Epihodov, mind you see everything is right.

EPIHODOV (*in a husky voice*). Don't you trouble, Yermolay Alexeyevitch.

LOPAHIN. Why, what's wrong with your voice?

EPIHODOV. I've just had a drink of water, and I choked over something.

YASHA (*contemptuously*). The ignorance!

LYUBOV. We are going—and not a soul will be left here.

LOPAHIN. Not till the spring.

VARYA (*pulls a parasol out of a bundle, as though about to hit someone with it.* LOPAHIN *makes a gesture as though alarmed*). What is it? I didn't mean anything.

TROFIMOV. Ladies and gentlemen, let us get

into the carriage. It's time. The train will be in directly.

VARYA. Petya, here they are, your goloshes, by that box. (*With tears*) And what dirty old things they are!

TROFIMOV (*putting on his goloshes*). Let us go, friends!

GAEV (*greatly agitated, afraid of weeping*). The train—the station! Double baulk, ah!

LYUBOV. Let us go!

LOPAHIN. Are we all here? (*locks the side-door on left*). The things are all here. We must lock up. Let us go!

ANYA. Good-bye, home! Good-bye to the old life!

TROFIMOV. Welcome to the new life!

(TROFIMOV *goes out with* ANYA. VARYA *looks round the room and goes out slowly.* YASHA *and* CHARLOTTA IVANOVNA, *with her dog, go out.*)

LOPAHIN. Till the spring, then! Come, friends, till we meet! (*goes out*).

(LYUBOV ANDREYEVNA *and* GAEV *remain alone. As though they had been waiting for this, they throw themselves on each other's necks, and break into subdued smothered sobbing, afraid of being overheard.*)

GAEV (*in despair*). Sister, my sister!

LYUBOV. Oh, my orchard!—my sweet, beautiful orchard! My life, my youth, my happiness, good-bye! good-bye!

VOICE OF ANYA (*calling gaily*). Mamma!

VOICE OF TROFIMOV (*gaily, excitedly*). Aa—oo!

LYUBOV. One last look at the walls, at the

windows. My dear mother loved to walk about this room.

GAEV. Sister, sister!

VOICE OF ANYA. Mamma!

VOICE OF TROFIMOV. Aa—oo!

LYUBOV. We are coming. (*They go out.*)

(*The stage is empty. There is the sound of the doors being locked up, then of the carriages driving away. There is silence. In the stillness there is the dull stroke of an axe in a tree, clanging with a mournful lonely sound. Footsteps are heard.* FIRS *appears in the doorway on the right. He is dressed as always—in a pea-jacket and white waistcoat, with slippers on his feet. He is ill.*)

FIRS (*goes up to the doors, and tries the handles*). Locked! They have gone . . . (*sits down on sofa*). They have forgotten me. . . . Never mind . . . I'll sit here a bit. . . . I'll be bound Leonid Andreyevitch hasn't put his fur coat on and has gone off in his thin overcoat (*sighs anxiously*). I didn't see after him. . . . These young people . . . (*mutters something that can't be distinguished*). Life has slipped by as though I hadn't lived. (*Lies down*) I'll lie down a bit. . . . There's no strength in you, nothing left you—all gone! Ech! I'm good for nothing (*lies motionless*).

(*A sound is heard that seems to come from the sky, like a breaking harp-string, dying away mournfully. All is still again, and there is heard nothing but the strokes of the axe far away in the orchard.*)

CURTAIN.

UNCLE VANYA

SCENES FROM COUNTRY LIFE, IN FOUR ACTS

First performed in 1899.

CHARACTERS IN THE PLAY

ALEXANDR VLADIMIROVITCH SEREBRYAKOV (*a retired Professor*).
YELENA ANDREYEVNA (*his wife, aged 27*).
SOFYA ALEXANDROVNA (SONYA) (*his daughter by his first wife*).
MARYA VASSILYEVNA VOYNITSKY (*widow of a Privy Councillor and mother of Professor's first wife*).
IVAN PETROVITCH VOYNITSKY (*her son*).
MIHAIL LVOVITCH ASTROV (*a Doctor*).
ILYA ILYITCH TELYEGIN (*a Landowner reduced to poverty*).
MARINA (*an old Nurse*).
A LABOURER.

The action takes place on SEREBRYAKOV'S *estate*

ACT I

Garden. Part of the house can be seen with the verandah. In the avenue under an old poplar there is a table set for tea. Garden seats and chairs; on one of the seats lies a guitar. Not far from the table there is a swing. Between two and three o'clock on a cloudy afternoon.

MARINA, *a heavy old woman, slow to move, is sitting by the samovar, knitting a stocking, and* ASTROV *is walking up and down near her.*

MARINA (*pours out a glass of tea*). Here, drink it, my dear.

ASTROV (*reluctantly takes the glass*). I don't feel much like it.

MARINA. Perhaps you would have a drop of vodka?

ASTROV. No. I don't drink vodka every day. Besides, it's so sultry (*a pause*). Nurse, how many years have we known each other?

MARINA (*pondering*). How many? The Lord help my memory. . . . You came into these parts . . . when? Vera Petrovna, Sonitchka's mother, was living then. You came to see us two winters before she died. . . . Well, that must be eleven years ago. (*After a moment's thought*) Maybe even more. . . .

ASTROV. Have I changed much since then?

MARINA. Very much. You were young and handsome in those days, and now you have grown older. And you are not as good-looking. There's another thing too—you take a drop of vodka now.

ASTROV. Yes. . . . In ten years I have become a different man. And what's the reason of it? I am overworked, nurse. From morning till night I am always on my legs, not a moment of rest, and at night one lies under the bedclothes in continual terror of being dragged out to a patient. All these years that you have known me I have not had one free day. I may well look old! And the life in itself is tedious, stupid, dirty. . . . This life swallows one up completely. There are none but queer people about one—they are a queer lot, all of them—and when one has lived two or three years among them, by degrees one turns queer too, without noticing it. It's inevitable (*twisting his long moustache*). Ough, what a huge moustache I've grown . . . a stupid moustache. . . . I've turned into a queer fish, nurse. I haven't grown stupid yet, thank God! My brains are in their place, but my feelings are somehow blunter. There is nothing I want, nothing I care about, no one I am fond of . . . except you, perhaps—I am fond of you (*kisses her on the head*). I had a nurse like you when I was a child.

MARINA. Perhaps you would like something to eat?

ASTROV. No. In the third week of Lent I went to Malitskoe, where there was an epidemic . . . spotted typhus . . . in the huts the people were lying about in heaps. There was filth, stench, smoke . . . calves on the ground with the sick . . . little pigs about too. I was hard at work all day, did not sit down for a minute, and hadn't a morsel of food, and when I got home they wouldn't let me rest. They brought me a signal-man from the line. I laid him on the table to operate upon him, and he went and died under the chloroform. And just when they weren't wanted, my feelings seemed to wake up again, and I was as conscience-stricken as though I had killed him on purpose. I sat down, shut my eyes like this, and thought: those who will live a hundred or two hundred years after us, for whom we are struggling now to beat out a road, will they remember and say a good word for us? Nurse, they won't, you know!

MARINA. Men will not remember, but God will remember.

ASTROV. Thank you for that. That's a good saying.

(*Enter* VOYNITSKY.)

VOYNITSKY (*comes out of the house; he has had a nap after lunch and looks rumpled; he sits down on the garden-seat and straightens his fashionable tie*). Yes . . . (*a pause*). Yes. . . .

ASTROV. Had a good sleep?

VOYNITSKY. Yes . . . very (*yawns*). Ever since the Professor and his wife have been here our life has been turned topsy-turvy. I sleep at the wrong time, at lunch and dinner I eat all sorts of messes, I drink wine—it's not good for one! In old days I never had a free moment. Sonya and I used to work in grand style, but now Sonya works alone, while I sleep and eat and drink. It's bad!

MARINA (*shaking her head*). Such goings-on! The Professor gets up at twelve o'clock, and the samovar is boiling all the morning waiting for him. Before they came we always had dinner about one o'clock, like other people, and now they are here we have it between six and seven. The Professor spends the night reading and writing, and all at once, at two o'clock in the morning, he'll ring his bell. Goodness me! What is it? Tea! People have to be waked out of their sleep to get him the samovar. What goings-on!

ASTROV. And will they be here much longer?

VOYNITSKY (*whistles*). A hundred years. The Professor has made up his mind to settle here.

MARINA. Look now! The samovar has been on the table for the last two hours, and they've gone for a walk.

VOYNITSKY. They are coming. They are coming! Don't worry.

(*There is a sound of voices; from the farther part of the garden enter* SEREBRYAKOV, YELENA ANDREYEVNA, SONYA *and* TELYEGIN *returning from a walk.*)

SEREBRYAKOV. Lovely, lovely! . . . Exquisite views!

TELYEGIN. Remarkable, your Excellency.

SONYA. We'll go to the plantation to-morrow, father. Shall we?

VOYNITSKY. Tea is ready!

SEREBRYAKOV. My friends, be so kind as to send

my tea into the study for me. I have something more I must do to-day.

SONYA. You will be sure to like the plantation.

(YELENA ANDREYEVNA, SEREBRYAKOV, *and* SONYA *go into the house.* TELYEGIN *goes to the table and sits down beside* MARINA.)

VOYNITSKY. It's hot, stifling; but our great man of learning is in his greatcoat and goloshes, with an umbrella and gloves too.

ASTROV. That shows that he takes care of himself.

VOYNITSKY. And how lovely she is! How lovely! I've never seen a more beautiful woman.

TELYEGIN. Whether I drive through the fields, Marina Timofyevna, or walk in the shady garden, or look at this table, I feel unutterably joyful. The weather is enchanting, the birds are singing, we are all living in peace and concord—what more could one wish for? (*taking his glass*). I am truly grateful to you!

VOYNITSKY (*dreamily*). Her eyes . . . an exquisite woman!

ASTROV. Tell us something, Ivan Petrovitch.

VOYNITSKY (*listlessly*). What am I to tell you?

ASTROV. Is there nothing new?

VOYNITSKY. Nothing. Everything is old. I am just as I always was, perhaps worse, for I have grown lazy. I do nothing but just grumble like some old crow. My old magpie *Maman* is still babbling about the rights of women. With one foot in the grave, she is still rummaging in her learned books for the dawn of a new life.

ASTROV. And the Professor?

VOYNITSKY. The Professor, as before, sits in his study writing from morning till dead of night. "With furrowed brow and racking brains, We write and write and write, And ne'er a word of praise we hear, Our labours to requite." Poor paper! He had much better be writing his autobiography. What a superb subject! A retired professor, you know—an old dry-as-dust, a learned fish. Gout, rheumatism, migraine, envy and jealousy have affected his liver. The old fish is living on his first wife's estate, living there against his will because he can't afford to live in the town. He is forever complaining of his misfortunes, though, as a matter of fact, he is exceptionally fortunate. (*Nervously*) Just think how fortunate! The son of a humble sacristan, he has risen to university distinctions and the chair of a professor; he has become "your Excellency," the son-in-law of a senator, and so on, and so on. All that is no great matter, though. But just take this. The man has been lecturing and writing about art for twenty-five years, though he knows absolutely nothing about art. For twenty-five years he has been chewing over other men's ideas about realism, naturalism, and all sorts of nonsense; for twenty-five years he has been lecturing and writing on things all intelligent people know about already and stupid ones aren't interested in—so for twenty-five years he has been simply wasting his time. And with all that, what conceit! What pretensions! He has retired, and not a living soul knows anything about him; he is absolutely unknown. So that for twenty-five years all he has done is to keep a better man out of a job! But just look at him: he struts about like a demi-god!

ASTROV. Come, I believe you are envious.

VOYNITSKY. Yes, I am. And the success he has with women! Don Juan is not in it. His first wife, my sister, a lovely, gentle creature, pure as this blue sky, noble, generous, who had more suitors than he has had pupils, loved him as only pure angels can love beings as pure and beautiful as themselves. My mother adores him to this day, and he still inspires in her a feeling of devout awe. His second wife, beautiful, intelligent—you have just seen her—has married him in his old age, sacrificed her youth, her beauty, her freedom, her brilliance, to him. What for? Why?

ASTROV. Is she faithful to the Professor?

VOYNITSKY. Unhappily, she is.

ASTROV. Why unhappily?

VOYNITSKY. Because that fidelity is false from beginning to end. There is plenty of fine sentiment in it, but no logic. To deceive an old husband whom one can't endure is immoral; but to try and stifle her piteous youth and living feeling—that's not immoral.

TELYEGIN (*in a tearful voice*). Vanya, I can't bear to hear you talk like that. Come, really! Anyone who can betray wife or husband is a person who can't be trusted and who might betray his country.

VOYNITSKY (*with vexation*). Dry up, Waffles!

TELYEGIN. Excuse me, Vanya. My wife ran away from me with the man she loved the day after our wedding, on the ground of my unprepossessing appearance. But I have never been false to my vows. I love her to this day and am faithful to her. I help her as far as I can, and I gave all I had for the education of her children by the man she loved. I have lost my happiness, but my pride has been left to me. And she? Her youth is over, her beauty, in accordance with the laws of nature, has faded, the man she loved is dead. . . . What has she left?

(*Enter* SONYA *and* YELENA ANDREYEVNA *and a little later,* MARYA VASSILYEVNA *with a book; she sits down and reads. They hand her tea, and she drinks it without looking at it.*)

SONYA (*hurriedly to the nurse*). Nurse, darling, some peasants have come. Go and speak to them. I'll look after the tea.

(*Exit Nurse.* YELENA ANDREYEVNA *takes her cup and drinks it sitting in the swing.*)

ASTROV (*to* YELENA ANDREYEVNA). I've come to see your husband. You wrote to me that he was very ill—rheumatism and something else—but it appears he is perfectly well.

YELENA. Last night he was poorly, complaining of pains in his legs, but to-day he is all right. . . .

ASTROV. And I have galloped twenty miles at break-neck speed! But there, it doesn't matter! it's not the first time. I shall stay with you till to-morrow to make up for it, and anyway I shall sleep *quantum satis.*

SONYA. That's splendid! It's not often you stay the night with us. I expect you've not had dinner?

ASTROV. No, I haven't.

SONYA. Oh, well, you will have some dinner, then! We have dinner now between six and seven (*drinks tea*). The tea is cold!

TELYEGIN. The temperature in the samovar has perceptibly dropped.

YELENA. Never mind, Ivan Ivanitch; we will drink it cold.

TELYEGIN. I beg your pardon, I am not Ivan Ivanitch, but Ilya Ilyitch—Ilya Ilyitch Telyegin, or, as some people call me on account of my pock-marked face, Waffles. I stood godfather to Sonetchka, and his Excellency, your husband, knows me very well. I live here now on your estate. If you've been so kind as to observe it, I have dinner with you every day.

SONYA. Ilya Ilyitch is our helper, our right hand. (*Tenderly*) Let me give you another cup, godfather.

MARYA. Ach!

SONYA. What is it, grandmamma?

MARYA. I forgot to tell Alexandr—I am losing my memory—I got a letter to-day from Harkov, from Pavel Alexeyevitch . . . he has sent his new pamphlet.

ASTROV. Is it interesting?

MARYA. It's interesting, but it's rather queer. He is attacking what he himself maintained seven years ago. It's awful.

VOYNITSKY. There's nothing awful in it. Drink your tea, *maman*.

MARYA. But I want to talk.

VOYNITSKY. But we have been talking and

talking for fifty years and reading pamphlets. It's about time to leave off.

MARYA. You don't like listening when I speak; I don't know why. Forgive my saying so, Jean, but you have so changed in the course of the last year that I hardly know you. You used to be a man of definite principles, of elevating ideas.

VOYNITSKY. Oh, yes! I was a man of elevating ideas which elevated nobody (*a pause*). . . . A man of elevating ideas . . . you could not have made a more malignant joke! Now I am forty-seven. Till last year I tried, like you, to blind myself with all your pedantic rubbish on purpose to avoid seeing life as it is—and thought I was doing the right thing. And now, if only you knew! I can't sleep at night for vexation, for rage that I so stupidly wasted the time when I might have had everything from which my age now shuts me out.

SONYA. Uncle Vanya, it's so dreary!

MARYA (*to her son*). You seem to be blaming your former principles. It is not they that are to blame, but yourself. You forget that principles alone are no use—a dead letter. You ought to have been working.

VOYNITSKY. Working? It is not everyone who can be a writing machine like your Herr Professor.

MARYA. What do you mean by that?

SONYA (*in an imploring voice*). Grandmamma! Uncle Vanya! I entreat you!

VOYNITSKY. I'll hold my tongue—hold my tongue and apologise.

(*A pause.*)

YELENA. What a fine day! It's not too hot.

(*A pause.*)

VOYNITSKY. A fine day to hang oneself!

(TELYEGIN *tunes the guitar.* MARINA *walks to and fro near the house, calling a hen.*)

MARINA. Chook, chook, chook!

SONYA. Nurse, darling, what did the peasants come about?

MARINA. It's the same thing—about the waste land again. Chook, chook, chook!

SONYA. Which is it you are calling?

MARINA. Speckly has gone off somewhere with her chickens. . . . The crows might get them (*walks away*).

(TELYEGIN *plays a polka; they all listen to him in silence. Enter a labourer.*)

LABOURER. Is the doctor here? (*To* ASTROV) If you please, Mihail Lvovitch, they have sent for you.

ASTROV. Where from?

LABOURER. From the factory.

ASTROV (*with vexation*). Much obliged to you. Well, I suppose I must go (*looks round him for his cap*). What a nuisance, hang it!

SONYA. How annoying it is, really! Come back from the factory to dinner.

ASTROV. No. It will be too late. "How should I? . . . How could I? . . ." (*To the labourer*) Here, my good man, you might get me a glass of vodka, anyway. (*Labourer goes off.*) "How should I? . . . How could I? . . ." (*finds his cap*). In one of Ostrovsky's plays there is a man with a big moustache and little wit—that's like me. Well,

I have the honour to wish you all good-bye. (*To* YELENA ANDREYEVNA) If you ever care to look in upon me, with Sofya Alexandrovna, I shall be truly delighted. I have a little estate, only ninety acres, but there is a model garden and nursery such as you wouldn't find for hundreds of miles round—if that interests you. Next to me is the government plantation. The forester there is old and always ill, so that I really look after all the work.

YELENA. I have been told already that you are very fond of forestry. Of course, it may be of the greatest use, but doesn't it interfere with your real work ? You are a doctor.

ASTROV. Only God knows what is one's real work.

YELENA. And is it interesting ?

ASTROV. Yes, it is interesting work.

VOYNITSKY (*ironically*). Very much so !

YELENA (*to* ASTROV). You are still young—you don't look more than thirty-six or thirty-seven . . . and it cannot be so interesting as you say. Nothing but trees and trees. I should think it must be monotonous.

SONYA. No, it's extremely interesting. Mihail Lvovitch plants fresh trees every year, and already they have sent him a bronze medal and a diploma. He tries to prevent the old forests being destroyed. If you listen to him you will agree with him entirely. He says that forests beautify the country, that they teach man to understand what is beautiful and develop a lofty attitude of mind. Forests temper the severity of the climate.

In countries where the climate is mild, less energy is wasted on the struggle with nature, and so man is softer and milder. In such countries people are beautiful, supple and sensitive ; their language is elegant and their movements are graceful. Art and learning flourish among them, their philosophy is not gloomy, and their attitude to women is full of refined courtesy.

VOYNITSKY (*laughing*). Bravo, bravo ! That's all charming but not convincing ; so (*to* ASTROV) allow me, my friend, to go on heating my stoves with logs and building my barns of wood.

ASTROV. You can heat your stoves with peat and build your barns of brick. Well, I am ready to let you cut down wood as you need it, but why destroy the forests ? The Russian forests are going down under the axe. Millions of trees are perishing, the homes of wild animals and birds are being laid waste, the rivers are dwindling and drying up, wonderful scenery is disappearing never to return ; and all because lazy man has not the sense to stoop down and pick up the fuel from the ground. (*To* YELENA ANDREYEVNA) Am I not right, madam ? One must be an unreflecting savage to burn this beauty in one's stove, to destroy what we cannot create. Man is endowed with reason and creative force to increase what has been given him ; but hitherto he has not created but destroyed. There are fewer and fewer forests, the rivers are drying up, the wild creatures are becoming extinct, the climate is ruined, and every day the earth is growing poorer and more hideous. (*To* VOYNITSKY) Here you are looking at me with irony, and all I say seems to you not serious and—perhaps I really am a crank. But when I walk by the peasants' woods which I have saved from cutting down, or when I hear the rustling of the young copse planted by my own hands, I realise that the climate is to some extent in my power, and that if in a thousand years man is to be happy I too shall have had some small hand in it. When I plant a birch tree and see it growing green and swaying in the wind my soul is filled with pride, and I . . . (*seeing the labourer, who has brought a glass of vodka on a tray*). However (*drinks*), it's time for me to go. Probably the truth of the matter is that I am a crank. I have the honour to take my leave! (*goes towards the house*).

SONYA (*takes his arm and goes with him*). When are you coming to us?

ASTROV. I don't know.

SONYA. Not for a month again?

(ASTROV *and* SONYA *go into the house;* MARYA VASSILYEVNA *and* TELYEGIN *remain at the table;* YELENA ANDREYEVNA *walks towards the verandah.*)

YELENA. You have been behaving impossibly again, Ivan Petrovitch. Why need you have irritated Marya Vassilyevna and talked about a writing machine! And at lunch to-day you quarrelled with Alexandr again. How petty it is!

VOYNITSKY. But if I hate him?

YELENA. There is no reason to hate Alexandr; he is like everyone else. He is no worse than you are.

VOYNITSKY. If you could see your face, your movements! You are too indolent to live! Ah, how indolent!

YELENA. Ach! indolent and bored! Everyone abuses my husband; everyone looks at me with compassion, thinking, "Poor thing! she has got an old husband." This sympathy for me, oh, how well I understand it! As Astrov said just now, you all recklessly destroy the forests, and soon there will be nothing left on the earth. In just the same way you recklessly destroy human beings, and soon, thanks to you, there will be no fidelity, no purity, no capacity for sacrifice left on earth! Why is it you can never look with indifference at a woman unless she is yours? Because—that doctor is right—there is a devil of destruction in all of you. You have no feeling for the woods, nor the birds, nor for women, nor for one another!

VOYNITSKY. I don't like this moralising.

(*A pause.*)

YELENA. That doctor has a weary, sensitive face. An interesting face. Sonya is evidently attracted by him; she is in love with him, and I understand her feeling. He has come three times since I have been here, but I am shy and have not once had a proper talk with him, or been nice to him. He thinks I am disagreeable. Most likely that's why we are such friends, Ivan Petrovitch, that we are both such tiresome, tedious people. Tiresome! Don't look at me like that, I don't like it.

VOYNITSKY. How else can I look at you, since

I love you? You are my happiness, my life, my youth! I know the chances of your returning my feeling are nil, non-existent, but I want nothing, only let me look at you, listen to your voice. . . .

YELENA. Hush, they may hear you! (*They go into the house.*)

VOYNITSKY (*following her*). Let me speak of my love, don't drive me away—that alone will be the greatest happiness for me. . . .

YELENA. This is agonising.

(*Both go into the house.* TELYEGIN *strikes the strings and plays a polka.* MARYA VASSILYEVNA *makes a note on the margin of a pamphlet.*)

CURTAIN.

ACT II

Dining-room in SEREBRYAKOV'S *house. Night. A watchman can be heard tapping in the garden.* SEREBRYAKOV, *sitting in an arm-chair before an open window, dozing, and* YELENA ANDREYEVNA *sitting beside him, dozing too.*

SEREBRYAKOV (*waking*). Who is it? Sonya, is it you?

YELENA. It's me.

SEREBRYAKOV. You, Lenotchka! . . . I am in unbearable pain.

YELENA. Your rug has fallen on the floor (*wrapping it round his legs*). I'll shut the window, Alexandr.

SEREBRYAKOV. No, I feel suffocated. . . . I just dropped asleep and I dreamed that my left leg did not belong to me. I was awakened by the agonising pain. No, it's not gout; it's more like rheumatism. What time is it now?

YELENA. Twenty minutes past twelve (*a pause*).

SEREBRYAKOV. Look for Batyushkov in the library in the morning. I believe we have his works.

YELENA. What?

SEREBRYAKOV. Look for Batyushkov in the morning. I remember we did have him. But why is it so difficult for me to breathe?

YELENA. You are tired. This is the second night you have not slept.

SEREBRYAKOV. I have been told that Turgenev got *angina pectoris* from gout. I am afraid I may have it. Hateful, detestable old age. Damnation take it! Since I have grown old I have grown hateful to myself. And you must all hate the sight of me.

YELENA. You talk of your age as though we were all responsible for it.

SEREBRYAKOV. I am most of all hateful to you.

(YELENA ANDREYEVNA *gets up and sits down farther away.*)

SEREBRYAKOV. Of course, you are right. I am not a fool, and I understand. You are young and strong and good-looking. You want life and I am an old man, almost a corpse. Do you suppose I don't understand? And, of course, it is stupid of me to go on living. But wait a little, I shall soon set you all free. I shan't have to linger on much longer.

YELENA. I am worn out . . . for God's sake be quiet!

SEREBRYAKOV. It seems that, thanks to me, everyone is worn out, depressed, wasting their youth, and I am the only one enjoying life and satisfied. Oh yes, of course!

YELENA. Be quiet! You make me miserable!

SEREBRYAKOV. I make everyone miserable. Of course.

YELENA (*through tears*). It's insufferable! Say, what is it you want of me?

SEREBRYAKOV. Nothing.

YELENA. Well, be quiet then. I implore you!

SEREBRYAKOV. It's a strange thing, Ivan Petrovitch may speak and that old idiot, Marya Vassilyevna, and there is nothing against it, everyone listens—but if I say a word everyone begins to feel miserable. They dislike the very sound of my voice. Well, suppose I am disagreeable, egoistic and tyrannical—haven't I a right, even in my old age, to think of myself? Haven't I earned it? Haven't I the right, I ask you, to be quiet in my old age, to be cared for by other people?

YELENA. No one is disputing your rights. (*The window bangs in the wind.*) The wind has got up; I'll shut the window (*shuts the window*). There will be rain directly. No one disputes your rights.

(*A pause; the watchman in the garden taps and sings.*)

SEREBRYAKOV. After devoting all one's life to learning, after growing used to one's study, to one's lecture-room, to the society of honourable colleagues—all of a sudden to find oneself here in this vault, every day to see stupid people, to hear foolish conversation. I want life, I like success, I like fame, I like distinction, renown, and here—it's like being an exile. Every moment to be grieving for the past, watching the successes of others, dreading death. I can't bear it! It's too much for me! And then they won't forgive me my age!

YELENA. Wait a little, have patience: in five or six years I shall be old too.

(*Enter* SONYA.)

SONYA. Father, you told us to send for Doctor Astrov yourself, and now that he has come you won't see him. It isn't nice. You've troubled him for nothing.

SEREBRYAKOV. What good is your Astrov to me? He knows as much about medicine as I do about astronomy.

SONYA. We can't send for all the great medical authorities here for your gout.

SEREBRYAKOV. I am not going to talk to that crazy crank.

SONYA. That's as you please (*sits down*). It doesn't matter to me.

SEREBRYAKOV. What's the time?

YELENA. Nearly one o'clock.

SEREBRYAKOV. I feel stifled. . . . Sonya, fetch me my drops from the table.

SONYA. In a minute (*gives him the drops*).

SEREBRYAKOV (*irritably*). Oh, not those! It's no use asking for anything!

SONYA. Please don't be peevish. Some people may like it, but please spare me! I don't like it. And I haven't the time. I have to get up early in the morning, we are haymaking to-morrow.

(*Enter* VOYNITSKY *in a dressing-gown with a candle in his hand.*)

VOYNITSKY. There's a storm coming on. (*A flash of lightning.*) There, look! Hélène and Sonya, go to bed. I have come to take your place.

SEREBRYAKOV (*frightened*). No, no! Don't leave me with him No! He will be the death of me with his talking!

VOYNITSKY. But you must let them have some

rest! This is the second night they have had no sleep.

SEREBRYAKOV. Let them go to bed, but you go too. Thank you. I entreat you to go. For the sake of our past friendship, don't make any objections! We'll talk some other time.

VOYNITSKY (*mockingly*). Our past friendship. . . . Past . . .

SONYA. Be quiet, Uncle Vanya.

SEREBRYAKOV (*to his wife*). My love, don't leave me alone with him! He will be the death of me with his talking!

VOYNITSKY. This is really getting laughable.

(*Enter* MARINA *with a candle.*)

SONYA. You ought to be in bed, nurse darling! It's late.

MARINA. The samovar has not been cleared. One can't very well go to bed.

SEREBRYAKOV. Everyone is kept up, everyone is worn out. I am the only one enjoying myself.

MARINA (*going up to* SEREBRYAKOV *tenderly*). Well, master dear, is the pain so bad? I have a grumbling pain in my legs too, such a pain (*tucks the rug in*). You've had this trouble for years. Vera Petrovna, Sonetchka's mother, used to be up night after night with you, wearing herself out. How fond she was of you! (*a pause*). The old are like little children, they like someone to be sorry for them; but no one feels for the old (*kisses* SEREBRYAKOV *on the shoulder*). Come to bed, dear . . . come, my honey. . . . I'll give you some lime-flower tea and warm your legs . . . and say a prayer for you. . . .

SEREBRYAKOV (*moved*). Let us go, Marina.

MARINA. I have such a grumbling pain in my legs myself, such a pain (*together with* SONYA *leads him off*). Vera Petrovna used to be crying, and breaking her heart over you. . . . You were only a mite then, Sonetchka, and had no sense. . . . Come along, come along, sir . . .

(SEREBRYAKOV, SONYA *and* MARINA *go out.*)

YELENA. I am quite worn out with him. I can hardly stand on my feet.

VOYNITSKY. You with him, and I with myself. This is the third night I have had no sleep.

YELENA. It's dreadful in this house. Your mother hates everything except her pamphlets and the Professor; the Professor is irritated, he does not trust me, and is afraid of you; Sonya is angry with her father, angry with me and has not spoken to me for a fortnight; you hate my husband and show open contempt for your mother; I am overwrought and have been nearly crying twenty times to-day. . . . It's dreadful in this house.

VOYNITSKY. Let us drop this moralising.

YELENA. You are a well-educated and intelligent man, Ivan Petrovitch, and I should have thought you ought to understand that the world is not being destroyed through fire or robbery, but through hatred, enmity and all this petty wrangling. . . . It ought to be your work to reconcile everyone, and not to grumble.

VOYNITSKY. Reconcile me to myself first! My precious . . . (*bends down and kisses her hand*).

YELENA. Don't! (*draws away her hand*). Go away!

VOYNITSKY. The rain will be over directly and everything in nature will be refreshed and sigh with relief. But the storm has brought no relief to me. Day and night the thought that my life has been hopelessly wasted weighs on me like a nightmare. I have no past, it has been stupidly wasted on trifles, and the present is awful in its senselessness. Here you have my life and my love! What use to make of them? What am I to do with them? My passion is wasted in vain like a ray of sunshine that has fallen into a pit, and I am utterly lost, too.

YELENA. When you talk to me about your love, I feel stupid and don't know what to say. Forgive me, there is nothing I can say to you (*is about to go out*). Good-night.

VOYNITSKY (*barring her way*). And if you knew how wretched I am at the thought that by my side, in this same house, another life is being wasted, too—yours! What are you waiting for? What cursed theory holds you back? Understand, do understand . . .

YELENA (*looks at him intently*). Ivan Petrovitch, you are drunk!

VOYNITSKY. I may be, I may be . . .

YELENA. Where is the doctor?

VOYNITSKY. He is in there . . . he is staying the night with me. It may be, it may be . . . anything may be!

YELENA. You have been drinking again to-day. What's that for?

VOYNITSKY. There's a semblance of life in it, anyway. . . . Don't prevent me, Hélène!

YELENA. You never used to drink, and you did not talk so much. . . . Go to bed! You bore me.

VOYNITSKY (*kisses her hand*). My precious . . . marvellous one!

YELENA (*with vexation*). Don't. This is really hateful (*goes out*).

VOYNITSKY (*alone*). She is gone . . . (*a pause*). Ten years ago I used to meet her at my sister's. Then she was seventeen and I was thirty-seven. Why didn't I fall in love with her then and make her an offer? It might easily have happened then! And now she would have been my wife. . . . Yes. . . . Now we should both have been awakened by the storm; she would have been frightened by the thunder, I should have held her in my arms and whispered, "Don't be frightened, I am here." Oh, wonderful thoughts, what happiness; it makes me laugh with delight—but, my God, my thoughts are in a tangle. Why am I old? Why doesn't she understand me? Her fine phrases, her lazy morality, her nonsensical lazy theories about the ruin of the world—all that is absolutely hateful to me (*a pause*). Oh, how I have been cheated! I adored that Professor, that pitiful gouty invalid, and worked for him like an ox. Sonya and I squeezed every farthing out of the estate; we haggled over linseed oil, peas, curds, like greedy peasants; we grudged ourselves every morsel to save up halfpence and farthings and send him thousands of roubles. I was proud of him and his learning; he was my life, the breath of my being. All his writings and utterances seemed to me inspired by genius. . . . My God, and now!

Here he is retired, and now one can see the sum total of his life. He leaves not one page of work behind him, he is utterly unknown, he is nothing—a soap bubble! And I have been cheated. . . . I see it—stupidly cheated. . . .

(*Enter* ASTROV *in his coat, but without waistcoat or tie; he is a little drunk; he is followed by* TELYEGIN *with the guitar.*)

ASTROV. Play something!

TELYEGIN. Everyone is asleep!

ASTROV. Play!

(TELYEGIN *begins playing softly.*)

ASTROV (*to* VOYNITSKY). Are you alone? No ladies here? (*Putting his arms akimbo sings*) "Dance my hut and dance my stove, the master has no bed to lie on." The storm woke me. Jolly good rain. What time is it?

VOYNITSKY. Goodness knows.

ASTROV. I thought I heard Yelena Andreyevna's voice.

VOYNITSKY. She was here a minute ago.

ASTROV. A fine woman. (*Examines the medicine bottles on the table*) Medicines! What a lot of prescriptions! From Harkov, from Moscow, from Tula. He has bored every town with his gout. Is he really ill or shamming?

VOYNITSKY. He is ill (*a pause*).

ASTROV. Why are you so melancholy to-day? Are you sorry for the Professor, or what?

VOYNITSKY. Let me alone.

ASTROV. Or perhaps you are in love with the Professor's lady?

VOYNITSKY. She is my friend!

ASTROV. Already?

VOYNITSKY. What do you mean by "already"?

ASTROV. A woman can become a man's friend only in the following sequence: first agreeable acquaintance, then mistress, then friend

VOYNITSKY. A vulgar theory.

ASTROV. What? Yes . . . I must own I am growing vulgar. You see, I am drunk too. As a rule I get drunk like this once a month. When I am in this condition I become coarse and insolent in the extreme. I don't stick at anything then! I undertake the most difficult operations and do them capitally. I make the most extensive plans for the future; I don't think of myself as a crank at such times, but believe that I am being of immense service to humanity—immense! And I have my own philosophy of life at such times, and all you, my good friends, seem to me such insects . . . microbes! (*To* TELYEGIN) Waffles, play!

TELYEGIN. My dear soul, I'd be delighted to do anything for you, but do realise—everyone is asleep!

ASTROV. Play!

(TELYEGIN *begins playing softly.*)

ASTROV. We must have a drink. Come along, I fancy we have still some brandy left. And as soon as it is daylight, we will go to my place. Right? I have an assistant who never says "right," but "roight." He is an awful scoundrel. So we will go, shall we? (*Sees* SONYA *entering*) Excuse me, I have no tie on (*goes out hurriedly,* TELYEGIN *following him*).

SONYA. Uncle Vanya, you have been drinking

with the doctor again. You are a nice pair! He has always been like that, but why do you do it? It's so unsuitable at your age.

VOYNITSKY. Age makes no difference. When one has no real life, one has to live on illusions. It's better than nothing, anyway.

SONYA. The hay is all cut, it rains every day, it's all rotting, and you are living in illusions. You have quite given up looking after things. . . . I have to work alone, and am quite done up. . . . (*Alarmed*) Uncle, you have tears in your eyes!

VOYNITSKY. Tears? Not a bit of it . . . nonsense. . . . You looked at me just now so like your dear mother. My darling . . . (*eagerly kisses her hands and face*). My sister . . . my dear sister . . . where is she now? If she knew! Ah, if she knew!

SONYA. What, uncle? Knew what?

VOYNITSKY. It's painful, useless. . . . Never mind. . . . Afterwards . . . it's nothing . . . I am going (*goes out*).

SONYA (*knocks at the door*). Mihail Lvovitch, you are not asleep, are you? One minute!

ASTROV (*through the door*). I am coming! (*A minute later he comes out with his waistcoat and tie on.*) What can I do for you?

SONYA. Drink yourself, if it does not disgust you, but I implore you, don't let my uncle drink! It's bad for him.

ASTROV. Very good. We won't drink any more (*a pause*). I am just going home. That's settled and signed. It will be daylight by the time they have put the horses in.

SONYA. It is raining. Wait till morning.

ASTROV. The storm is passing over, we shall only come in for the end of it. I'm going. And please don't send for me again to see your father. I tell him it's gout and he tells me it's rheumatism; I ask him to stay in bed and he sits in a chair. And to-day he wouldn't speak to me at all.

SONYA. He is spoiled. (*Looks into the sideboard*) Won't you have something to eat?

ASTROV. Well, perhaps.

SONYA. I like eating at night. I believe there is something in the sideboard. They say he's been a great favourite with the ladies, and women have spoiled him. Here, have some cheese. (*Both stand at the sideboard and eat.*)

ASTROV. I have had nothing to eat all day, only drink. Your father has a difficult temper. (*Takes a bottle from the sideboard*) May I? (*drinks a glass*). There is no one here and one may speak frankly. Do you know, it seems to me that I could not exist in your house for a month, I should be choked by the atmosphere. . . . Your father, who is entirely absorbed in his gout and his books, Uncle Vanya with his melancholy, your grandmother, and your stepmother too. . . .

SONYA. What about my stepmother?

ASTROV. Everything ought to be beautiful in a human being: face, and dress, and soul, and ideas. She is beautiful, there is no denying that, but . . . You know she does nothing but eat, sleep, walk about, fascinate us all by her beauty —nothing more. She has no duties, other people work for her. . . . That's true, isn't it? And an idle life cannot be pure (*a pause*). But perhaps I am too severe. I am dissatisfied with life like your Uncle Vanya, and we are both growing peevish.

SONYA. You are dissatisfied with life, then?

ASTROV. I love life as such, but our life, our everyday provincial life in Russia, I can't endure. I despise it with every fibre of my being. And as for my own personal life, there is absolutely nothing nice in it, I can assure you. You know when you walk through a forest on a dark night, and a light gleams in the distance, you do not notice your weariness, nor the darkness, nor the sharp twigs that lash you in the face. . . . I work—as you know—harder than anyone in the district, fate is for ever lashing at me; at times I am unbearably miserable, but I have no light in the distance. I expect nothing for myself; I am not fond of my fellow creatures. . . . It's years since I cared for anyone.

SONYA. You care for no one at all?

ASTROV. No one. I feel a certain affection for your nurse—for the sake of old times. The peasants are too much alike, undeveloped, living in dirt, and it is difficult to get on with the educated people. They are all wearisome. Our good friends are small in their ideas, small in their feelings, and don't see beyond their noses—or, to put it plainly, they are stupid. And those who are bigger and more intelligent are hysterical, morbidly absorbed in introspection and analysis. . . . They are for ever whining; they are insanely given to hatred and slander; they steal up to a man sideways, and look at him askance and decide "Oh, he is a neurotic!" or "he is posing."

And when they don't know what label to stick on my forehead, they say "he is a queer fellow, very queer!" I am fond of forestry—that's queer; I don't eat meat—that's queer too. There is no direct, genuine, free attitude to people and to nature left among them. . . . None, none! (*is about to drink*).

SONYA (*prevents him*). No, please, I beg you, don't drink any more!

ASTROV. Why not?

SONYA. It's so out of keeping with you! You are so refined, you have such a soft voice. . . . More than that even, you are unlike everyone else I know—you are beautiful. Why, then, do you want to be like ordinary people who drink and play cards? Oh, don't do it, I entreat you! You always say that people don't create but only destroy what heaven gives them. Then why do you destroy yourself, why? You mustn't, you mustn't, I beseech you, I implore you!

ASTROV (*holds out his hand to her*). I won't drink any more!

SONYA. Give me your word.

ASTROV. My word of honour.

SONYA (*presses his hand warmly*). Thank you!

ASTROV. Enough! I have come to my senses. You see, I am quite sober now and I will be so to the end of my days (*looks at his watch*). And so, as I was saying, my time is over, it's too late for me. . . . I have grown old, I have worked too hard, I have grown vulgar, all my feelings are blunted, and I believe I am not capable of being fond of anyone. I don't love anyone . . . and I don't believe I ever shall. What still affects me is beauty. That does stir me. I fancy if Yelena Andreyevna, for example, wanted to, she could turn my head in one day. . . . But that's not love, that's not affection . . . (*covers his face with his hands and shudders*).

SONYA. What is it?

ASTROV. Nothing. . . . In Lent one of my patients died under chloroform.

SONYA. You ought to forget that by now (*a pause*). Tell me, Mihail Lvovitch . . . if I had a friend or a younger sister, and if you found out that she . . . well, suppose that she loved you, how would you take that?

ASTROV (*shrugging his shoulders*). I don't know. Nohow, I expect. I should give her to understand that I could not care for her . . . and my mind is taken up with other things. Anyway, if I am going, it is time to start. Good-bye, my dear girl, or we shall not finish till morning (*presses her hand*). I'll go through the drawing-room if I may, or I am afraid your uncle may detain me (*goes out*).

SONYA (*alone*). He has said nothing to me. . . . His soul and his heart are still shut away from me, but why do I feel so happy? (*laughs with happiness*). I said to him, you are refined, noble, you have such a soft voice. . . . Was it inappropriate? His voice trembles and caresses one . . . I still feel it vibrating in the air. And when I spoke to him of a younger sister, he did not understand. . . . (*Wringing her hands*) Oh, how awful it is that I am not beautiful! How awful it is! And I know I am not, I know it, I know it! . . . Last Sunday, as people were coming out of church, I heard them talking about me, and one woman said: "She is a sweet generous nature, but what a pity she is so plain. . . ." Plain. . . .

(*Enter* YELENA ANDREYEVNA.)

YELENA (*opens the window*). The storm is over. What delicious air! (*a pause*). Where is the doctor?

SONYA. He is gone (*a pause*).

YELENA. Sophie!

SONYA. What is it?

YELENA. How long are you going to be sulky with me? We have done each other no harm. Why should we be enemies? Let us make it up. . . .

SONYA. I wanted to myself . . . (*embraces her*). Don't let us be cross any more.

YELENA. That's right. (*Both are agitated.*)

SONYA. Has father gone to bed?

YELENA. No, he is sitting in the drawing-room. . . . We don't speak to each other for weeks, and goodness knows why. . . . (*Seeing that the sideboard is open*) How is this?

SONYA. Mihail Lvovitch has been having some supper.

YELENA. And there is wine too. . . . Let us drink to our friendship.

SONYA. Yes, let us.

YELENA. Out of the same glass . . . (*fills it*). It's better so. So now we are friends?

SONYA. Friends. (*They drink and kiss each other.*) I have been wanting to make it up for ever so long, but somehow I felt ashamed . . . (*cries*).

YELENA. Why are you crying ?

SONYA. It's nothing.

YELENA. Come, there, there . . . (*weeps*). I am a queer creature, I am crying too . . . (*a pause*). You are angry with me because you think I married your father from interested motives. . . . If that will make you believe me, I will swear it—I married him for love. I was attracted by him as a learned, celebrated man. It was not real love, it was all made up; but I fancied at the time that it was real. It's not my fault. And ever since our marriage you have been punishing me with your clever, suspicious eyes.

SONYA. Come, peace! peace! Let us forget.

YELENA. You mustn't look like that—it doesn't suit you. You must believe in everyone—there is no living if you don't (*a pause*.)

SONYA. Tell me honestly, as a friend . . . are you happy ?

YELENA. No.

SONYA. I knew that. One more question. Tell me frankly, wouldn't you have liked your husband to be young ?

YELENA. What a child you are still! Of course I should! (*laughs*). Well, ask something else, ask away. . . .

SONYA. Do you like the doctor ?

YELENA. Yes, very much.

SONYA (*laughs*). Do I look silly . . . yes ? He has gone away, but I still hear his voice and his footsteps, and when I look at the dark window I can see his face. Do let me tell you. . . . But I can't speak so loud; I feel ashamed. Come into my room, we can talk there. You must think me silly? Own up. . . . Tell me something about him.

YELENA. What am I to tell you?

SONYA. He is clever. . . . He understands everything, he can do anything. . . . He doctors people, and plants forests too. . . .

YELENA. It is not a question of forests and medicine. . . . My dear, you must understand he has a spark of genius! And you know what that means? Boldness, freedom of mind, width of outlook. . . . He plants a tree and is already seeing what will follow from it in a thousand years, already he has visions of the happiness of humanity. Such people are rare, one must love them. . . . He drinks, he is sometimes a little coarse—but what does that matter? A talented man cannot keep spotless in Russia. Only think what sort of life that doctor has! Impassable mud on the roads, frosts, snow-storms, the immense distances, the coarse savage peasants, poverty and disease all around him—it is hard for one who is working and struggling day after day in such surroundings to keep spotless and sober till he is forty (*kisses her*). I wish you happiness with all my heart; you deserve it . . . (*gets up*). But I am a tiresome, secondary character. . . . In music and in my husband's house, and in all the love affairs, everywhere in fact, I have always played a secondary part. As a matter of fact, if you come to think of it, Sonya, I am very, very unhappy! (*walks up and down the stage in agitation*). There is no happiness in this world for me, none! Why do you laugh?

SONYA (*laughs, hiding her face*). I am so happy . . . so happy!

YELENA. I have a longing for music. I should like to play something.

SONYA. Do play something! (*embraces her*). I can't sleep. . . . Play something!

YELENA. In a minute. Your father is not asleep. Music irritates him when he is ill. Go and ask his leave. If he doesn't object, I'll play. Go!

SONYA. Very well (*goes out*).

(*Watchman taps in the garden.*)

YELENA. It's a long time since I have played the piano. I shall play and cry, cry like an idiot. (*In the window*) Is that you tapping, Yefim?

WATCHMAN'S VOICE. Yes.

YELENA. Don't tap, the master is unwell.

WATCHMAN'S VOICE. I am just going (*whistles*). Hey there, good dog! Come, lad! Good dog! (*a pause*).

SONYA (*returning*). We mustn't!

CURTAIN.

ACT III

The drawing-room in SEREBRYAKOV'S *house. Three doors: on the right, on the left and in the middle. Daytime.*

VOYNITSKY *and* SONYA *seated, and* YELENA ANDREYEVNA *walking about the stage, thinking.*

VOYNITSKY. The Herr Professor has graciously expressed a desire that we should all gather together in this room at one o'clock to-day (*looks at his watch*). It is a quarter to. He wishes to make some communication to the world.

YELENA. Probably some business matter.

VOYNITSKY. He has no business. He spends his time writing twaddle, grumbling and being jealous.

SONYA (*in a reproachful tone*). Uncle!

VOYNITSKY. Well, well, I am sorry (*motioning towards* YELENA ANDREYEVNA). Just look at her! she is so lazy that she almost staggers as she walks. Very charming! Very!

YELENA. You keep buzzing and buzzing away all day—aren't you tired of it? (*Miserably*) I am bored to death. I don't know what I'm to do.

SONYA (*shrugging her shoulders*). Isn't there plenty to do? If only you cared to do it.

YELENA. For instance?

SONYA. You could help us with the estate, teach

the children or look after the sick. There's plenty to do. When father and you were not here, Uncle Vanya and I used to go to the market ourselves and sell the flour.

YELENA. I don't know how to do such things. And they are not interesting. It's only in novels with a purpose that people teach and doctor the peasants. How am I, all of a sudden, *à propos* of nothing, to go and teach them or doctor them?

SONYA. Well, I don't see how one can help doing it. Wait a little, and you too will get into the way of it (*puts her arm round her*). Don't be depressed, dear (*laughs*). You are bored and don't know what to do with yourself, and boredom and idleness are catching. Look at Uncle Vanya—he does nothing but follow you about like a shadow. I have left my work and run away to talk to you. I have grown lazy—I can't help it! The doctor, Mihail Lvovitch, used to come and see us very rarely, once a month; it was difficult to persuade him to come, and now he drives over every day. He neglects his forestry and his patients. You must be a witch.

VOYNITSKY. Why be miserable? (*Eagerly*) Come, my precious, my splendid one, be sensible! You have mermaid blood in your veins—be a mermaid! Let yourself go for once in your life! Make haste and fall head over ears in love with some water-sprite—and plunge headlong into the abyss so that the Herr Professor and all of us may throw up our hands in amazement!

YELENA (*angrily*). Leave me in peace! How cruel it is! (*is about to go out*).

VOYNITSKY (*prevents her*). Come, come, my dearest, forgive me. . . . I apologise (*kisses her hand*). Peace!

YELENA. You would drive an angel out of patience, you know.

VOYNITSKY. As a sign of peace and harmony I'll fetch you a bunch of roses; I gathered them for you this morning. Autumn roses—exquisite, mournful roses . . . (*goes out*).

SONYA. Autumn roses — exquisite, mournful roses. . . . (*Both look out of window.*)

YELENA. It's September already. However are we to get through the winter here? (*a pause*). Where is the doctor?

SONYA. In Uncle Vanya's room. He is writing something. I am glad Uncle Vanya is gone. I want to talk to you.

YELENA. What about?

SONYA. What about! (*lays her head on* YELENA'S *bosom*).

YELENA. Come, there, there . . . (*strokes her head*).

SONYA. I am not good-looking.

YELENA. You have beautiful hair.

SONYA. No! (*looks round so as to see herself in the looking-glass*). No! When a woman is plain, she is always told "You have beautiful eyes, you have beautiful hair." . . . I have loved him for six years. I love him more than my own mother. Every moment I am conscious of him. I feel the touch of his hand and I watch the door. I wait, expecting him every moment to come in. And here you see I keep coming to you simply to talk of him. Now he is here every day, but he doesn't look at me—doesn't see me. . . . That's such agony!

I have no hope at all—none, none! (*In despair*) Oh, my God, give me strength. . . . I have been praying all night. . . . I often go up to him, begin talking to him, look into his eyes. I have no pride left, no strength to control myself. I couldn't keep it in and told Uncle Vanya yesterday that I love him. . . . And all the servants know I love him. Everybody knows it.

YELENA. And he?

SONYA. No. He doesn't notice me.

YELENA (*musing*). He is a strange man. . . . Do you know what? Let me speak to him. . . . I'll do it carefully—hint at it . . . (*a pause*). Yes really—how much longer are you to remain in uncertainty? Let me!

(SONYA *nods her head in consent.*)

YELENA. That's right. It won't be difficult to find out whether he loves you or not. Don't you be troubled, darling; don't be uneasy. I'll question him so tactfully that he won't notice it. All we want to find out is yes or no (*a pause*). If it's no, he had better not come here, had he?

(SONYA *nods in agreement.*)

YELENA. It's easier to bear when one doesn't see the man. We won't put things off; we will question him straight away. He was meaning to show me some charts. Go and tell him that I want to see him.

SONYA (*in violent agitation*) You will tell me the whole truth?

YELENA. Yes, of course. It seems to me that the truth, however dreadful it is, is not so dreadful as uncertainty. Rely on me, dear.

SONYA. Yes, yes . . . I shall tell him you want to

see his charts (*is going, and stops in the doorway*). No, uncertainty is better. . . . One has hope, at least. . . .

YELENA. What do you say?

SONYA. Nothing (*goes out*).

YELENA (*alone*). Nothing is worse than knowing somebody else's secret and not being able to help. (*Musing*) He is not in love with her—that's evident; but why should he not marry her? She is not good-looking, but she would be a capital wife for a country doctor at his age. She is so sensible, so kind and pure-hearted. . . . No, that's not it . . . (*a pause*). I understand the poor child. In the midst of desperate boredom, with nothing but grey shadows wandering about instead of human beings, with only dull commonplaces to listen to, among people who can do nothing but eat, drink and sleep—he sometimes appears on the scene unlike the rest, handsome, interesting, fascinating, like a bright moon rising in the darkness. . . . To yield to the charm of such a man . . . forget oneself . . . I believe I am a little fascinated myself. Yes, I feel bored when he does not come, and even now I am smiling when I think of him. . . . That Uncle Vanya says I have mermaid's blood in my veins. "Let yourself go for once in your life." Well, perhaps that's what I ought to do. . . . If I could fly, free as a bird, away from all of you—from your sleepy faces, from your talk, forget your existence. . . . But I am cowardly and diffident. . . . My conscience troubles me. . . . He comes here every day. I guess why he comes, and already I have a guilty feeling. I am ready to throw myself on my knees before Sonya, to beg her pardon, to cry. . . .

ASTROV (*comes in with a chart*). Good-day! (*shakes hands*). You wanted to see my handiwork.

YELENA. You promised yesterday to show me. . . . Can you spare the time?

ASTROV. Oh, of course! (*spreads the map on a card table and fixes it with drawing pins*). Where were you born?

YELENA (*helping him*). In Petersburg.

ASTROV. And where did you study?

YELENA. At the School of Music.

ASTROV. I expect this won't be interesting to you.

YELENA. Why not? It's true that I don't know the country, but I have read a great deal.

ASTROV. I have my own table here, in this house . . . in Ivan Petrovitch's room. When I am so exhausted that I feel completely stupefied, I throw everything up and fly here and amuse myself with this for an hour or two. . . . Ivan Petrovitch and Sofya Alexandrovna click their counting beads, and I sit beside them at my table and daub away—and I feel snug and comfortable, and the cricket churrs. But I don't allow myself that indulgence too often—only once a month. . . . (*Pointing to the map*) Now, look here! It's a picture of our district as it was fifty years ago. The dark and light green stands for forest; half of the whole area was covered with forest. Where there is a network of red over the green, elks and wild goats were common. . . . I show both the flora and the fauna here. On this lake there were swans, geese and ducks, and the old people tell us there were "a power " of birds of all sorts, no end of them ; they flew in clouds. Besides the villages and hamlets, you see scattered here and there all sorts of settlements—little farms, monasteries of Old Believers, water-mills. . . . Horned cattle and horses were numerous. That is shown by the blue colour. For instance, the blue colour lies thick on this neighbourhood. Here there were regular droves of horses, and every homestead had three on an average (*a pause*). Now look lower down. That's how it was twenty-five years ago. Already, you see, only a third of the area is under forest. There are no goats left, but there are elks. Both the green and the blue are paler. And so it goes on and on. Let us pass to the third part—a map of the district as it is at present. There is green here and there, but only in patches ; all the elks have vanished, and the swans and the capercailzies too. . . . Of the old settlements and farms and monasteries and mills there is not a trace. In fact, it's a picture of gradual and unmistakable degeneration which will, apparently, in another ten or fifteen years be complete. You will say that it is the influence of civilisation—that the old life must naturally give way to the new. Yes, I understand that. If there were highroads and railways on the site of these ruined forests, if there were works and factories and schools, the peasants would be healthier, better off, more intelligent ; but, you see, there is nothing of the sort ! There are still the same swamps and mosquitoes, the same lack of roads, and poverty, and typhus and diphtheria and fires in the district. . . .

We have here a degeneration that is the result of too severe a struggle for existence. This degeneration is due to inertia, ignorance, to the complete lack of understanding, when a man, cold, hungry and sick, simply to save what is left of life, to keep his children alive, instinctively, unconsciously clutches at anything to satisfy his hunger and warm himself and destroys everything heedless of the morrow. . . . Almost everything has been destroyed already, but nothing as yet has been created to take its place. (*Coldly*) I see from your face that it doesn't interest you.

YELENA. But I understand so little about all that. . . .

ASTROV. There's nothing to understand in it ; it simply doesn't interest you.

YELENA. To speak frankly, I am thinking of something else. Forgive me. I want to put you through a little examination, and I am troubled and don't know how to begin.

ASTROV. An examination ?

YELENA. Yes, an examination . . . but not a very formidable one. Let us sit down. (*They sit down.*) It concerns a certain young lady. We will talk like honest people, like friends, without beating about the bush. Let us talk and forget all about it afterwards. Yes ?

ASTROV. Yes.

YELENA. It concerns my step-daughter Sonya. You like her, don't you ?

ASTROV. Yes, I have a respect for her.

YELENA. Does she attract you as a woman ?

ASTROV (*after a pause*). No.

YELENA. A few words more, and I have done. Have you noticed nothing?

ASTROV. Nothing.

YELENA (*taking him by the hand*). You do not love her . . . I see it from your eyes. . . . She is unhappy. . . . Understand that and . . . give up coming here.

ASTROV (*gets up*). My day is over. Besides, I have too much to do (*shrugging his shoulders*). What time have I for such things? (*he is confused*).

YELENA. Ough! What an unpleasant conversation! I am trembling as though I'd been carrying a ton weight. Well, thank God, that's over! Let us forget it. Let it be as though we had not spoken at all, and . . . and go away. You are an intelligent man . . . you'll understand (*a pause*). I feel hot all over.

ASTROV. If you had spoken a month or two ago I might, perhaps, have considered it; but now . . . (*he shrugs his shoulders*). And if she is unhappy, then of course . . . There's only one thing I can't understand: what induced you to go into it? (*Looks into her eyes and shakes his finger at her*) You are a sly one!

YELENA. What does that mean?

ASTROV (*laughs*). Sly! Suppose Sonya is unhappy—I am quite ready to admit it—but why need you go into it? (*Preventing her from speaking, eagerly*) Please don't try to look astonished. You know perfectly well what brings me here every day. . . . Why, and on whose account, I am here, you know perfectly well. You charming bird of prey, don't look at me like that, I am an old sparrow. . . .

YELENA (*perplexed*). Bird of prey! I don't understand.

ASTROV. A beautiful, fluffy weasel. . . . You must have a victim ! Here I have been doing nothing for a whole month. I have dropped everything. I seek you greedily—and you are awfully pleased at it, awfully. . . . Well, I am conquered ; you knew that before your examination (*folding his arms and bowing his head*). I submit. Come and devour me !

YELENA. You are mad !

ASTROV (*laughs through his teeth*). You—diffident. . . .

YELENA. Oh, I am not so bad and so mean as you think ! I swear I'm not ! (*tries to go out*).

ASTROV (*barring the way*). I am going away to-day. I won't come here again, but . . . (*takes her hand and looks round*) where shall we see each other ? Tell me quickly, where ? Someone may come in ; tell me quickly. . . . (*Passionately*) How wonderful, how magnificent you are ! One kiss. . . . If I could only kiss your fragrant hair. . . .

YELENA. I assure you . . .

ASTROV (*preventing her from speaking*). Why assure me ? There's no need. No need of unnecessary words. . . . Oh, how beautiful you are ! What hands ! (*kisses her hands*).

YELENA. That's enough . . . go away . . . (*withdraws her hands*). You are forgetting yourself.

ASTROV. Speak, speak ! Where shall we meet to-morrow ? (*puts his arm round her waist*). You see, it is inevitable ; we must meet (*kisses her ; at that instant* VOYNITSKY *comes in with a bunch of roses and stands still in the doorway*)

YELENA (*not seeing* VOYNITSKY). Spare me . . . let me go . . . (*lays her head on* ASTROV'S *chest*). No ! (*tries to go out*).

ASTROV (*holding her by the waist*). Come to the plantation to-morrow . . . at two o'clock. . . . Yes? Yes? You'll come?

YELENA (*seeing* VOYNITSKY). Let me go! (*in extreme confusion goes to the window*). This is awful!

VOYNITSKY (*lays the roses on a chair; in confusion wipes his face and his neck with his handkerchief*). Never mind . . . no . . . never mind. . . .

ASTROV (*carrying it off with bravado*). The weather is not so bad to-day, honoured Ivan Petrovitch. It was overcast in the morning, as though we were going to have rain, but now it is sunny. To tell the truth, the autumn has turned out lovely . . . and the winter corn is quite promising (*rolls up the map*). The only thing is the days are getting shorter . . . (*goes out*).

YELENA (*goes quickly up to* VOYNITSKY). You will try—you will do your utmost that my husband and I should leave here to-day! Do you hear? This very day

VOYNITSKY (*mopping his face*). What? Oh, yes . . . very well . . . I saw it all, Hélène—all. . . .

YELENA (*nervously*). Do you hear? I must get away from here to-day!

(*Enter* SEREBRYAKOV, TELYEGIN *and* MARINA.)

TELYEGIN. I don't feel quite the thing myself, your Excellency. I have been poorly for the last two days. My head is rather queer. . . .

SEREBRYAKOV. Where are the others? I don't like this house. It's a perfect labyrinth. Twenty-six huge rooms, people wander in different directions, and there is no finding anyone (*rings*). Ask Marya Vassilyevna and Yelena Andreyevna to come here.

YELENA. I am here.

SEREBRYAKOV. I beg you to sit down, friends.

SONYA (*going up to* YELENA ANDREYEVNA, *impatiently*). What did he say?

YELENA. Presently.

SONYA. You are trembling! You are agitated! (*Looking searchingly into her face*) I understand. . . . He said that he won't come here again . . . yes? (*a pause*). Tell me: yes?

(YELENA ANDREYEVNA *nods.*)

SEREBRYAKOV (*to* TELYEGIN). One can put up with illness, after all; but what I can't endure is the whole manner of life in the country. I feel as though I had been cast off the earth into some other planet. Sit down, friends, I beg! Sonya! (*Sonya does not hear him; she stands with her head drooping sorrowfully*). Sonya! (*a pause*). She does not hear. (*To* MARINA) You sit down too, nurse. (*Nurse sits down, knitting a stocking.*) I beg you, my friends, hang your ears on the nail of attention, as the saying is (*laughs*).

VOYNITSKY (*agitated*). Perhaps I am not wanted? Can I go?

SEREBRYAKOV. No; it is you whom we need most.

VOYNITSKY. What do you require of me?

SEREBRYAKOV. Require of you. . . . Why are you

cross? (*a pause*). If I have been to blame in any way, pray excuse me.

VOYNITSKY. Drop that tone. Let us come to business. What do you want?

(*Enter* MARYA VASSILYEVNA.)

SEREBRYAKOV. Here is *maman*. I will begin, friends (*a pause*). I have invited you, gentlemen, to announce that the Inspector-General is coming. But let us lay aside jesting. It is a serious matter. I have called you together to ask for your advice and help, and, knowing your invariable kindness, I hope to receive it. I am a studious, bookish man, and have never had anything to do with practical life. I cannot dispense with the assistance of those who understand it, and I beg you, Ivan Petrovitch, and you, Ilya Ilyitch, and you, *maman*. . . . The point is that *manet omnes una nox*—that is, that we are all mortal. I am old and ill, and so I think it is high time to settle my worldly affairs so far as they concern my family. My life is over. I am not thinking of myself, but I have a young wife and an unmarried daughter (*a pause*). It is impossible for me to go on living in the country. We are not made for country life. But to live in town on the income we derive from this estate is impossible. If we sell the forest, for instance, that's an exceptional measure which we cannot repeat every year. We must take some steps which would guarantee us a permanent and more or less definite income. I have thought of such a measure, and have the honour of submitting it to your consideration. Omitting details I will put it before you in rough outline. Our estate yields on an average not more than two per cent. on its capital value. I propose to sell it. If we invest the money in suitable securities, we should get from four to five per cent., and I think we might even have a few thousand roubles to spare for buying a small villa in Finland.

VOYNITSKY. Excuse me . . . surely my ears are deceiving me! Repeat what you have said.

SEREBRYAKOV. To put the money in some suitable investment and with the remainder purchase a villa in Finland.

VOYNITSKY. Not Finland. . . . You said something else.

SEREBRYAKOV. I propose to sell the estate.

VOYNITSKY. That's it. You will sell the estate; superb, a grand idea. . . . And what do you propose to do with me, and your old mother and Sonya here?

SEREBRYAKOV. We will settle all that in due time. One can't go into everything at once.

VOYNITSKY. Wait a minute. It's evident that up to now I've never had a grain of common sense. Up to now I have always imagined that the estate belongs to Sonya. My father bought this estate as a dowry for my sister. Till now I have been simple; I did not interpret the law like a Turk, but thought that my sister's estate passed to Sonya.

SEREBRYAKOV. Yes, the estate belongs to Sonya. Who disputes it? Without Sonya's consent I shall not venture to sell it. Besides, I am proposing to do it for Sonya's benefit.

VOYNITSKY. It's inconceivable, inconceivable! Either I have gone out of my mind, or . . . or . . .

MARYA. Jean, don't contradict Alexandr. Believe me, he knows better than we do what is for the best.

VOYNITSKY. No; give me some water (*drinks water*). Say what you like—say what you like!

SEREBRYAKOV. I don't understand why you are so upset. I don't say that my plan is ideal. If everyone thinks it unsuitable, I will not insist on it.

(*A pause.*)

TELYEGIN (*in confusion*). I cherish for learning, your Excellency, not simply a feeling of reverence, but a sort of family feeling. My brother Grigory Ilyitch's wife's brother—perhaps you know him?—Konstantin Trofimitch Lakedemonov, was an M.A. . . .

VOYNITSKY. Stop, Waffles; we are talking of business. . . . Wait a little—later. . . . (*To* SEREBRYAKOV) Here, ask him. The estate was bought from his uncle.

SEREBRYAKOV. Oh! why should I ask him? What for?

VOYNITSKY. The estate was bought at the time for ninety-five thousand roubles. My father paid only seventy thousand, and twenty-five thousand remained on mortgage. Now, listen. . . . The estate would never have been bought if I had not renounced my share of the inheritance in favour of my sister, whom I loved dearly. What's more, I worked for ten years like a slave and paid off all the mortgage. . . .

SEREBRYAKOV. I regret that I broached the subject.

VOYNITSKY. The estate is free from debt and in a good condition only owing to my personal efforts. And now that I am old I am to be kicked out of it!

SEREBRYAKOV. I don't understand what you are aiming at.

VOYNITSKY. I have been managing this estate for twenty-five years. I have worked and sent you money like the most conscientious steward, and you have never thanked me once in all these years. All that time—both when I was young and now—you have given me five hundred roubles a year as salary—a beggarly wage!—and it never occurred to you to add a rouble to it.

SEREBRYAKOV. Ivan Petrovitch, how could I tell? I am not a practical man, and don't understand these things. You could have added as much to it as you chose.

VOYNITSKY. Why didn't I steal? How is it you don't all despise me because I didn't steal? It would have been right and I shouldn't have been a pauper now!

MARYA (*sternly*). Jean!

TELYEGIN (*in agitation*). Vanya, my dear soul, don't, don't . . . I am all of a tremble. . . . Why spoil our good relations? (*Kisses him*) You mustn't.

VOYNITSKY. For twenty-five years I have been here within these four walls with mother, buried like a mole. . . . All our thoughts and feelings belonged to you alone. By day we talked of you and your labours. We were proud of you; with reverence we uttered your name. We wasted our nights reading books and magazines for which now I have the deepest contempt !

TELYEGIN. Don't, Vanya, don't . . . I can't stand it. . . .

SEREBRYAKOV (*wrathfully*). I don't know what it is you want.

VOYNITSKY. To us you were a being of a higher order, and we knew your articles by heart. . . . But now my eyes are opened ! I see it all ! You write of art, but you know nothing about art ! All those works of yours I used to love are not worth a brass farthing ! You have deceived us !

SEREBRYAKOV. Do stop him ! I am going !

YELENA. Ivan Petrovitch, I insist on your being silent ! Do you hear ?

VOYNITSKY. I won't be silent. (*Preventing* SEREBRYAKOV *from passing*) Stay ! I have not finished. You have destroyed my life ! I have not lived ! I have not lived ! Thanks to you, I have ruined and wasted the best years of my life. You are my bitterest enemy.

TELYEGIN. I can't bear it . . . I can't bear it . . . I must go (*goes out, in violent agitation*).

SEREBRYAKOV. What do you want from me ? And what right have you to speak to me like this ? You nonentity ! If the estate is yours, take it. I don't want it !

YELENA. I am going away from this hell this very minute (*screams*). I can't put up with it any longer !

VOYNITSKY. My life is ruined ! I had talent, I had courage, I had intelligence ! If I had had a normal life I might have been a Schopenhauer, a Dostoevsky. . . . Oh, I am talking like an idiot! I am going mad. . . . Mother, I am in despair! Mother!

MARYA (*sternly*). Do as Alexandr tells you.

SONYA (*kneeling down before the nurse and huddling up to her*). Nurse, darling! Nurse, darling!

VOYNITSKY. Mother! What am I to do? Don't speak; there's no need! I know what I must do! (*To* SEREBRYAKOV) You shall remember me! (*goes out through middle door*).

(MARYA VASSILYEVNA *follows him.*)

SEREBRYAKOV. This is beyond everything! Take that madman away! I cannot live under the same roof with him. He is always there (*points to the middle door*)—almost beside me. . . . Let him move into the village, or into the lodge, or I will move; but remain in the same house with him I cannot. . . .

YELENA (*to her husband*). We will leave this place to-day! We must pack up this minute!

SEREBRYAKOV. An utterly insignificant creature!

SONYA (*on her knees, turns her head towards her father; hysterical through her tears*). You must be merciful, father! Uncle Vanya and I are so unhappy! (*Mastering her despair*) You must be merciful! Remember how, when you were younger, Uncle Vanya and grandmamma sat up all night translating books for you, copying your manuscripts . . . all night . . . all night . . . Uncle Vanya and I worked without resting—we were afraid to spend a farthing on ourselves and sent it all to you. . . . We did not eat the bread of idleness.

I am saying it all wrong—all wrong; but you ought to understand us, father. You must be merciful!

YELENA (*in agitation, to her husband*). Alexandr, for God's sake make it up with him. . . . I beseech you!

SEREBRYAKOV. Very well, I will talk to him. . . . I am not accusing him of anything, I am not angry with him. But you must admit that his behaviour is strange, to say the least of it. Very well, I'll go to him (*goes out by middle door*).

YELENA. Be gentle with him, soothe him . . . (*follows him out*).

SONYA (*hugging Nurse*). Oh, Nurse, darling! Nurse, darling!

MARINA. Never mind, child. The ganders will cackle a bit and leave off. . . . They will cackle and leave off. . . .

SONYA. Nurse, darling!

MARINA (*stroking her head*). You are shivering as though you were frozen! There, there, little orphan, God is merciful! A cup of lime-flower water, or raspberry tea, and it will pass. . . . Don't grieve, little orphan. (*Looking towards the middle door wrathfully*) What a to-do they make, the ganders! Plague take them!

(*A shot behind the scenes; a shriek from* YELENA ANDREYEVNA *is heard;* SONYA *shudders.*)

MARINA. Ough! Botheration take them!

SEREBRYAKOV (*runs in, staggering with terror*). Hold him! hold him! He is out of his mind!

(YELENA ANDREYEVNA *and* VOYNITSKY *struggle in the doorway.*)

YELENA (*trying to take the revolver from him*). Give it up! Give it up, I tell you!

VOYNITSKY. Let me go, Hélène! Let me go! (*Freeing himself from her, he runs in, looking for* SEREBRYAKOV) Where is he? Oh, here he is! (*Fires at him*) Bang! (*a pause*). Missed! Missed again! (*Furiously*) Damnation—damnation take it . . . (*flings revolver on the floor and sinks on to a chair, exhausted.* SEREBRYAKOV *is overwhelmed;* YELENA *leans against the wall, almost fainting*).

YELENA. Take me away! Take me away! Kill me . . . I can't stay here, I can't!

VOYNITSKY (*in despair*). Oh, what am I doing! What am I doing!

SONYA (*softly*). Nurse, darling! Nurse, darling!

CURTAIN.

ACT IV

VOYNITSKY'S *room: it is his bedroom and also his office. In the window there is a big table covered with account books and papers of all sorts; a bureau, bookcases, scales. A smaller table, for* ASTROV; *on that table there are paints and drawing materials; beside it a big portfolio. A cage with a starling in it. On the wall a map of Africa, obviously of no use to anyone. A big sofa covered with American leather. To the left a door leading to other apartments. On the right a door into the hall; near door, on right, there is a doormat, that the peasants may not muddy the floor. An autumn evening. Stillness.*

TELYEGIN *and* MARINA *sitting opposite each other winding wool.*

TELYEGIN. You must make haste, Marina Timofeyevna, they will soon be calling us to say good-bye. They have already ordered the horses.

MARINA (*tries to wind more rapidly*). There is not much left.

TELYEGIN. They are going to Harkov. They'll live there.

MARINA. Much better so.

TELYEGIN. They've had a fright. . . . Yelena

Andreyevna keeps saying, "I won't stay here another hour. Let us get away; let us get away." "We will stay at Harkov," she says; "we will have a look round and then send for our things. . . ." They are not taking much with them. It seems it is not ordained that they should live here, Marina Timofeyevna. It's not ordained. . . . It's the dispensation of Providence.

MARINA. It's better so. Look at the quarrelling and shooting this morning—a regular disgrace!

TELYEGIN. Yes, a subject worthy of the brush of Aïvazovsky.

MARINA. A shocking sight it was (*a pause*). We shall live again in the old way, as we used to. We shall have breakfast at eight, dinner at one, and sit down to supper in the evening; everything as it should be, like other people . . . like Christians (*with a sigh*). It's a long while since I have tasted noodles, sinner that I am!

TELYEGIN. Yes, it's a long time since they have given us noodles at dinner (*a pause*). A very long time. . . . As I was walking through the village this morning, Marina Timofeyevna, the man at the shop called after me, "You cadger, living upon other people." And it did hurt me so.

MARINA. You shouldn't take any notice of that, my dear. We all live upon God. Whether it's you or Sonya or Ivan Petrovitch, none of you sit idle, we all work hard! All of us. . . . Where is Sonya?

TELYEGIN. In the garden. She is still going round with the doctor looking for Ivan Petrovitch. They are afraid he may lay hands on himself.

MARINA. And where is his pistol?

TELYEGIN (*in a whisper*). I've hidden it in the cellar!

MARINA (*with a smile*). What goings on!

(*Enter* VOYNITSKY *and* ASTROV *from outside.*)

VOYNITSKY. Let me alone. (*To* MARINA *and* TELYEGIN) Go away, leave me alone—if only for an hour! I won't endure being watched.

TELYEGIN. Certainly, Vanya (*goes out on tiptoe*).

MARINA. The gander says, ga-ga-ga! (*gathers up her wool and goes out*).

VOYNITSKY. Let me alone!

ASTROV. I should be delighted to. I ought to have gone away ages ago, but I repeat I won't go till you give back what you took from me.

VOYNITSKY. I did not take anything from you.

ASTROV. I am speaking in earnest, don't detain me. I ought to have gone long ago.

VOYNITSKY. I took nothing from you. (*Both sit down.*)

ASTROV. Oh! I'll wait a little longer and then, excuse me, I must resort to force. We shall have to tie your hands and search you. I am speaking quite seriously.

VOYNITSKY. As you please (*a pause*). To have made such a fool of myself: to have fired twice and missed him! I shall never forgive myself for that.

ASTROV. If you wanted to be playing with firearms, you would have done better to take a pop at yourself.

VOYNITSKY (*shrugging his shoulders*). It's queer. I made an attempt to commit murder and I have not been arrested; no one has sent for the police. So I am looked upon as a madman (*with a bitter laugh*). I am mad, but people are not mad who hide their crass stupidity, their flagrant heartlessness under the mask of a professor, a learned sage. People are not mad who marry old men and then deceive them before the eyes of everyone. I saw you kissing her! I saw!

ASTROV. Yes, I did kiss her, and that's more than you ever have!

VOYNITSKY (*looking towards the door*). No, the earth is mad to let you go on living on it!

ASTROV. Come, that's silly.

VOYNITSKY. Well, I am mad. I am not responsible. I have a right to say silly things.

ASTROV. That's a stale trick. You are not a madman: you are simply a crank. A silly fool. Once I used to look upon every crank as an invalid—as abnormal; but now I think it is the normal condition of man to be a crank. You are quite normal.

VOYNITSKY (*covers his face with his hands*). I am ashamed! If you only knew how ashamed I am! No pain can be compared with this acute shame (*miserably*). It's unbearable (*bends over the table*). What am I to do? What am I to do?

ASTROV. Nothing.

VOYNITSKY. Give me something! Oh, my God! I am forty-seven. If I live to be sixty, I have another thirteen years. It's a long time! How am I to get through those thirteen years? What shall I do? How am I to fill them up? Oh, you know . . . (*squeezing* ASTROV'S *hand convulsively*); you know, if only one could live the remnant of one's life in some new way. Wake up on a still sunny morning and feel that one had begun a new life, that all the past was forgotten and had melted away like smoke (*weeps*). To begin a new life. . . . Tell me how to begin it . . . what to begin. . . .

ASTROV (*with vexation*). Oh, get away with you! New life, indeed! Our position—yours and mine—is hopeless.

VOYNITSKY. Yes?

ASTROV. I am convinced of it.

VOYNITSKY. Give me something. . . . (*Pointing to his heart*) I have a scalding pain here.

ASTROV (*shouts angrily*). Leave off! (*Softening*) Those who will live a hundred or two hundred years after us, and who will despise us for having lived our lives so stupidly and tastelessly—they will, perhaps, find a means of being happy; but we . . . There is only one hope for you and me. The hope that when we are asleep in our graves we may, perhaps, be visited by pleasant visions (*with a sigh*). Yes, old man, in the whole district there were only two decent, well-educated men: you and I. And in some ten years the common round of the trivial life here has swamped us, and has poisoned our life with its putrid vapours, and made us just as despicable as all the rest. (*Eagerly*) But don't try to put me off: give me what you took away from me.

VOYNITSKY. I took nothing from you.

ASTROV. You took a bottle of morphia out of my travelling medicine-chest (*a pause*). Look here, if you insist on making an end of yourself, go into the forest and shoot yourself. But give me back the morphia or else there will be talk and conjecture. People will think I have given it you. It will be quite enough for me to have to make your post-mortem. Do you think I shall find it interesting?

(*Enter* SONYA.)

VOYNITSKY. Leave me alone.

ASTROV (*to* SONYA). Sofya Alexandrovna, your uncle has taken a bottle of morphia out of my medicine-chest, and won't give it back. Tell him that it's . . . really stupid. And I haven't the time to waste. I ought to be going.

SONYA. Uncle Vanya, did you take the morphia? (*a pause*).

ASTROV. He did. I am certain of it.

SONYA. Give it back. Why do you frighten us? (*Tenderly*) Give it back, Uncle Vanya! I am just as unhappy, perhaps, as you are; but I am not going to give way to despair. I am bearing it, and will bear it, till my life ends of itself. . . . You must be patient too (*a pause*). Give it back! (*kisses his hands*). Dear, good uncle, darling! give it back! (*weeps*). You are kind, you will have pity on us and give it back. Be patient, uncle!—be patient!

VOYNITSKY (*takes the bottle out of the table-drawer and gives it to* ASTROV). There, take it! (*To* SONYA) But we must make haste and work, make haste and do something, or else I can't . . . I can't bear it.

SONYA. Yes, yes, work. As soon as we have seen our people off, we'll sit down to work. . . . (*Nervously turning over the papers on the table*) We have let everything go.

ASTROV (*puts the bottle into his case and tightens the straps*). Now I can set off.

(*Enter* YELENA.)

YELENA. Ivan Petrovitch, are you here? We are just starting. Go to Alexandr, he wants to say something to you.

SONYA. Go, Uncle Vanya. (*Takes* VOYNITSKY *by the arm*) Let us go. Father and you must be reconciled. That's essential.

(SONYA *and* VOYNITSKY *go out.*)

YELENA. I am going away. (*Gives* ASTROV *her hand*) Good-bye.

ASTROV. Already?

YELENA. The carriage is waiting.

ASTROV. Good-bye.

YELENA. You promised me to-day that you would go away.

ASTROV. I remember. I am just going (*a pause*). You have taken fright? (*takes her hand*). Is it so terrible?

YELENA. Yes.

ASTROV. You had better stay, after all! What do you say? To-morrow in the plantation——

YELENA. No. It's settled. And I look at you so fearlessly just because it is settled. I have only one favour to ask of you: think better of me. I should like you to have a respect for me.

ASTROV. Ugh! (*makes a gesture of impatience*). Do stay, I ask you to. Do recognise, you have nothing to do in this world, you have no object in life, you have nothing to occupy your mind, and sooner or later you will give way to feeling—it's inevitable. And it had better not be at

Harkov, or somewhere in Kursk, but here, in the lap of nature. . . . It's poetical, anyway, even the autumn is beautiful. . . . There is the forest plantation here, half-ruined homesteads in the Turgenev style. . . .

YELENA. How absurd you are. . . . I am angry with you, but yet . . . I shall think of you with pleasure. You are an interesting, original man. We shall never meet again, and so—why conceal i ?—I was really a little bit in love with you. Come, let us shake hands and part friends. Don't remember evil against me.

ASTROV (*pressing her hand*). Yes, you had better go . . . (*musing*). You seem to be a good, warm-hearted creature, and yet there is something strange about your whole personality, as it were. You came here with your husband, and all of us who were at work, toiling and creating something, had to fling aside our work and attend to nothing all the summer but your husband's gout and you. The two of you have infected all of us with your idleness. I was attracted by you and have done nothing for a whole month, and, meanwhile, people have been ill, and the peasants have pastured their cattle in my woods, of young, half-grown trees. . . . And so, wherever you and your husband go, you bring destruction everywhere. . . . I am joking, of course, yet . . . it is strange. And I am convinced that if you had stayed here, the devastation would have been immense. I should have been done for . . . and you wouldn't have fared well either ! Well, go away. *Finita la comedia* !

YELENA (*taking a pencil from his table and*

hurriedly putting it in her pocket). I shall take this pencil as a keepsake.

ASTROV. It is strange. . . . We have been friends and all at once for some reason . . . we shall never meet again. So it is with everything in this world. . . . While there is no one here—before Uncle Vanya comes in with a nosegay—allow me to kiss you at parting. . . . Yes? (*kisses her on the cheek*). That's right.

YELENA. I wish you all happiness. (*Looks round*) Well, so be it! For once in my life! (*embraces him impulsively and both simultaneously draw rapidly apart from each other*). I must go—I must go!

ASTROV. Make haste and go. Since the carriage is there, you had better set off.

YELENA. There's someone coming, I believe. (*Both listen.*)

ASTROV. *Finita!*

(*Enter* SEREBRYAKOV, VOYNITSKY, MARYA VASSILYEVNA, *with a book;* TELYEGIN *and* SONYA.)

SEREBRYAKOV (*to* VOYNITSKY). Let bygones be bygones. After what has happened, I have gone through and experienced so much in these few hours, that I believe I could write a whole treatise on the art of living for the benefit of posterity. I gladly accept your apologies and apologise myself. Good-bye! (*He and* VOYNITSKY *kiss each other three times.*)

VOYNITSKY. You shall receive regularly the same sum as hitherto. Everything shall be as before.

(YELENA ANDREYEVNA *embraces* SONYA.)

SEREBRYAKOV (*kisses* MARYA VASSILYEVNA'S *hand*). *Maman*. . . .

MARYA (*kissing him*). Alexandr, have your photograph taken again and send it to me. You know how dear you are to me.

TELYEGIN. Good-bye, your Excellency! Don't forget us!

SEREBRYAKOV (*kissing his daughter*). Good-bye . . . good-bye, everyone. (*Shaking hands with* ASTROV) Thanks for your pleasant company. I respect your way of thinking, your enthusiasms, your impulses, but permit an old man to add one observation to his farewell message: you must work, my friends! you must work! (*He bows to them all.*) I wish you all things good!

(*Goes out, followed by* MARYA VASSILYEVNA *and* SONYA.)

VOYNITSKY (*warmly kisses* YELENA ANDREYEVNA'S *hand*). Good-bye. . . . Forgive me. . . . We shall never meet again.

YELENA (*moved*). Good-bye, dear Ivan Petrovitch (*kisses him on the head and goes out*).

ASTROV (*to* TELYEGIN). Waffles, tell them, by the way, to bring my carriage round too.

TELYEGIN. Certainly, my dear soul (*goes out*).

(*Only* ASTROV *and* VOYNITSKY *remain.*)

ASTROV (*clearing his paints from the table and putting them away in his portmanteau*). Why don't you go and see them off?

VOYNITSKY. Let them go, I . . . I can't. My heart is too heavy. I must make haste and occupy myself with something. . . . Work! Work! (*rummages among his papers on the table*).

(*A pause; there is the sound of bells.*)

ASTROV. They've gone. The Professor is glad, I'll be bound. Nothing will tempt him back.

MARINA (*enters*). They've gone (*sits down in an easy chair and knits her stocking*).

SONYA (*enters*). They've gone (*wipes her eyes*). Good luck to them. (*To her uncle*) Well, Uncle Vanya, let us do something.

VOYNITSKY. Work, work. . . .

SONYA. It's ever so long since we sat at this table together (*lights the lamp on the table*). I believe there is no ink (*takes the inkstand, goes to the cupboard, and fills it with ink*). But I feel sad that they have gone.

(MARYA VASSILYEVNA *comes in slowly*.)

MARYA. They've gone (*sits down and becomes engrossed in reading*).

SONYA (*sits down to the table and turns over the pages of the account book*). First of all, Uncle Vanya, let us make out our accounts. We've neglected it all dreadfully. Someone sent for his account again to-day. Make it out. If you will do one account, I will do another.

VOYNITSKY (*writes*). "Delivered . . . to Mr. . . ." (*Both write in silence.*)

MARINA (*yawning*). I am ready for bye-bye.

ASTROV. How quiet it is! The pens scratch and the cricket churrs. It's warm and snug. I don't want to go. (*There is the sound of bells.*) There are my horses. . . . There is nothing left for me but to say good-bye to you, my friends—to say good-bye to my table—and be off! (*packs up his maps in the portfolio*).

MARINA. Why are you in such a hurry? You might as well stay.

ASTROV. I can't.

VOYNITSKY (*writes*). "Account delivered, two roubles and seventy-five kopecks."

(*Enter a* LABOURER.)

LABOURER. Mihail Lvovitch, the horses are ready.

ASTROV. I heard them. (*Hands him the medicine-chest, the portmanteau and the portfolio*) Here, take these. Mind you don't crush the portfolio.

LABOURER. Yes, sir.

ASTROV. Well? (*goes to say good-bye*).

SONYA. When shall we see you again?

ASTROV. Not before next summer, I expect. Hardly in the winter. . . . Of course, if anything happens, you'll let me know, and I'll come (*shakes hands*). Thank you for your hospitality, for your kindness—for everything, in fact. (*Goes up to nurse and kisses her on the head*) Good-bye, old woman.

MARINA. You are not going without tea?

ASTROV. I don't want any, nurse.

MARINA. Perhaps you'll have a drop of vodka?

ASTROV (*irresolutely*). Perhaps.

(MARINA *goes out.*)

ASTROV (*after a pause*). My trace-horse has gone a little lame. I noticed it yesterday when Petrushka was taking it to water.

VOYNITSKY. You must change his shoes.

ASTROV. I shall have to call in at the blacksmith's in Rozhdestvennoye. It can't be helped. (*Goes up to the map of Africa and looks at it*) I suppose in that Africa there the heat must be something terrific now!

VOYNITSKY. Yes, most likely.

MARINA (*comes back with a tray on which there is a glass of vodka and a piece of bread*). There you are.

(ASTROV *drinks the vodka.*)

MARINA. To your good health, my dear (*makes a low bow*). You should eat some bread with it.

ASTROV. No, I like it as it is. And now, good luck to you all. (*To* MARINA) Don't come out, nurse, there is no need.

(*He goes out;* SONYA *follows with a candle, to see him off;* MARINA *sits in her easy chair.*)

VOYNITSKY (*writes*). "February the second, Lenten oil, twenty pounds. February sixteenth, Lenten oil again, twenty pounds. Buckwheat . . ." (*a pause*).

(*The sound of bells.*)

MARINA. He has gone (*a pause*).

SONYA (*comes back and puts the candle on the table*). He has gone.

VOYNITSKY (*counts on the beads and writes down*). "Total . . . fifteen . . . twenty-five . . ."

(SONYA *sits down and writes.*)

MARINA (*yawns*). Lord have mercy on us!

(TELYEGIN *comes in on tiptoe, sits by the door and softly tunes the guitar.*)

VOYNITSKY (*to* SONYA, *passing his hand over her hair*). My child, how my heart aches! Oh, if only you knew how my heart aches!

SONYA. There is nothing for it. We must go on living! (*a pause*). We shall go on living, Uncle Vanya! We shall live through a long,

long chain of days and weary evenings; we shall patiently bear the trials which fate sends us; we shall work for others, both now and in our old age, and have no rest; and when our time comes we shall die without a murmur, and there beyond the grave we shall say that we have suffered, that we have wept, that life has been bitter to us, and God will have pity on us, and you and I, uncle, dear uncle, shall see a life that is bright, lovely, beautiful. We shall rejoice and look back at these troubles of ours with tenderness, with a smile—and we shall rest. I have faith, uncle; I have fervent, passionate faith. (*Slips on her knees before him and lays her head on his hands; in a weary voice*) We shall rest!

(TELYEGIN *softly plays on the guitar.*)

SONYA. We shall rest! We shall hear the angels; we shall see all Heaven lit with radiance; we shall see all earthly evil, all our sufferings, drowned in mercy which will fill the whole world, and our life will be peaceful, gentle and sweet as a caress. I have faith, I have faith (*wipes away his tears with her handkerchief*). Poor Uncle Vanya, you are crying. (*Through her tears*) You have had no joy in your life, but wait, Uncle Vanya, wait. We shall rest (*puts her arms round him*). We shall rest! (*The watchman taps.*)

(TELYEGIN *plays softly;* MARYA VASSILYEVNA *makes notes on the margin of her pamphlet;* MARINA *knits her stocking.*)

SONYA. We shall rest!

CURTAIN DROPS SLOWLY.

THE SEA-GULL

A COMEDY IN FOUR ACTS

First performed at St. Petersburg, October 17, 1896

CHARACTERS IN THE PLAY

IRINA NIKOLAYEVNA ARKADIN (MADAME TREPLEV) (*an Actress*).
KONSTANTIN GAVRILOVITCH TREPLEV (*her son, a young man*).
PYOTR NIKOLAYEVITCH SORIN (*her brother*).
NINA MIHAILOVNA ZARETCHNY (*a young girl, the daughter of a wealthy Landowner*).
ILYA AFANASYEVITCH SHAMRAEV (*a retired Lieutenant*, SORIN'S *Steward*).
POLINA ANDREYEVNA (*his wife*).
MASHA (*his daughter*).
BORIS ALEXEYEVITCH TRIGORIN (*a literary man*).
YEVGENY SERGEYEVITCH DORN (*a Doctor*).
SEMYON SEMYONOVITCH MEDVEDENKO (*a Schoolmaster*).
YAKOV (*a Labourer*).
A MAN COOK.
A HOUSEMAID.

The action takes place in SORIN'S *house and garden. Between the Third and the Fourth Acts there is an interval of two years.*

ACT I

Part of the park on SORIN'S *estate. Wide avenue leading away from the spectators into the depths of the park towards the lake is blocked up by a platform roughly put together for private theatricals, so that the lake is not visible. To right and left of the platform, bushes. A few chairs, a little table.*

The sun has just set. YAKOV *and other labourers are at work on the platform behind the curtain; there is the sound of coughing and hammering.* MASHA *and* MEDVEDENKO *enter on the left, returning from a walk.*

MEDVEDENKO. Why do you always wear black?

MASHA. I am in mourning for my life. I am unhappy.

MEDVEDENKO. Why? (*Pondering*) I don't understand. . . . You are in good health; though your father is not very well off, he has got enough. My life is much harder than yours. I only get twenty-three roubles a month, and from that they deduct something for the pension fund, and yet I don't wear mourning. (*They sit down.*)

MASHA. It isn't money that matters. A poor man may be happy.

MEDVEDENKO. Theoretically, yes; but in practice it's like this: there are my two sisters and my mother and my little brother and I, and my salary is only twenty-three roubles. We must eat and drink, mustn't we ? One must have tea and sugar. One must have tobacco. It's a tight fit.

MASHA (*looking round at the platform*). The play will soon begin.

MEDVEDENKO. Yes. Miss Zaretchny will act: it is Konstantin Gavrilitch's play. They are in love with each other and to-day their souls will be united in the effort to realise the same artistic effect. But your soul and mine have not a common point of contact. I love you. I am so wretched I can't stay at home. Every day I walk four miles here and four miles back and I meet with nothing but indifference from you. I can quite understand it. I am without means and have a big family to keep. . . . Who would care to marry a man who hasn't a penny to bless himself with ?

MASHA. Oh, nonsense ! (*takes a pinch of snuff*). Your love touches me, but I can't reciprocate it—that's all. (*Holding out the snuff-box to him*) Help yourself.

MEDVEDENKO. I don't feel like it (*a pause*).

MASHA. How stifling it is ! There must be a storm coming. . . . You're always discussing theories or talking about money. You think there is no greater misfortune than poverty, but to my mind it is a thousand times better to go in rags and be a beggar than . . . But you wouldn't understand that, though. . . .

(SORIN *and* TREPLEV *enter on the right.*)

SORIN (*leaning on his walking-stick*). I am never

quite myself in the country, my boy, and, naturally enough, I shall never get used to it. Last night I went to bed at ten and woke up this morning at nine feeling as though my brain were glued to my skull, through sleeping so long (*laughs*). And after dinner I accidentally dropped off again, and now I am utterly shattered and feel as though I were in a nightmare, in fact. . . .

TREPLEV. Yes, you really ought to live in town. (*Catches sight of* MASHA *and* MEDVEDENKO) When the show begins, my friends, you will be summoned, but you mustn't be here now. You must please go away.

SORIN (*to* MASHA). Marya Ilyinishna, will you be so good as to ask your papa to tell them to take the dog off the chain ?—it howls. My sister could not sleep again last night.

MASHA. Speak to my father yourself ; I am not going to. Please don't ask me. (*To* MEDVEDENKO) Come along !

MEDVEDENKO (*to* TREPLEV). So you will send and let us know before it begins. (*Both go out.*)

SORIN. So I suppose the dog will be howling all night again. What a business it is ! I have never done as I liked in the country. In old days I used to get leave for twenty-eight days and come here for a rest and so on, but they worried me so with all sorts of trifles that before I had been here two days I was longing to be off again (*laughs*). I've always been glad to get away from here. . . . But now I am on the retired list, and I have nowhere else to go, as a matter of fact. I've got to live here whether I like it or not. . . .

YAKOV (*to* TREPLEV). We are going to have a bathe, Konstantin Gavrilitch.

TREPLEV. Very well; but don't be more than ten minutes (*looks at his watch*). It will soon begin.

YAKOV. Yes, sir (*goes out*).

TREPLEV (*looking round the stage*). Here is our theatre. The curtain, then the first wing, then the second, and beyond that—open space. No scenery of any sort. There is an open view of the lake and the horizon. We shall raise the curtain at exactly half-past eight, when the moon rises.

SORIN. Magnificent.

TREPLEV. If Nina is late it will spoil the whole effect. It is time she was here. Her father and her stepmother keep a sharp eye on her, and it is as hard for her to get out of the house as to escape from prison (*puts his uncle's cravat straight*). Your hair and your beard are very untidy. They want clipping or something. . . .

SORIN (*combing out his beard*). It's the tragedy of my life. Even as a young man I looked as though I had been drinking for days or something of the sort. I was never a favourite with the ladies (*sitting down*). Why is your mother out of humour?

TREPLEV. Why? Because she is bored (*sitting down beside him*). She is jealous. She is set against me, and against the performance, and against my play because Nina is acting in it, and she is not. She does not know my play, but she hates it.

SORIN (*laughs*). What an idea!

TREPLEV. She is annoyed to think that even on this little stage Nina will have a triumph and not she (*looks at his watch*). My mother is a psychological freak. Unmistakably talented, intelligent, capable of sobbing over a book, she will reel off all Nekrassov by heart; as a sick nurse she is an angel; but just try praising Duse in her presence! O-ho! You must praise no one but herself, you must write about her, make a fuss over her, be in raptures over her extraordinary acting in "La Dame aux Camélias" or the "Ferment of Life"; but she has none of this narcotic in the country, she is bored and cross, and we are all her enemies—we are all in fault. Then she is superstitious—she is afraid of three candles, of the number thirteen. She is stingy. She has got seventy thousand roubles in a bank at Odessa—I know that for a fact—but ask her to lend you some money, and she will burst into tears.

SORIN. You imagine your mother does not like your play, and you are already upset and all that. Don't worry; your mother adores you.

TREPLEV (*pulling the petals off a flower*). Loves me, loves me not; loves me, loves me not; loves me, loves me not (*laughs*). You see, my mother does not love me. I should think not! She wants to live, to love, to wear light blouses; and I am twenty-five, and I am a continual reminder that she is no longer young. When I am not there she is only thirty-two, but when I am there she is forty-three, and for that she hates me. She knows, too, that I have no belief in the theatre. She loves the stage, she fancies she is working for humanity, for the holy cause of art, while to my mind the modern theatre is nothing but tradition and conventionality. When the curtain goes up, and by artificial light, in a room with three walls, these great geniuses, the devotees of holy art, represent how people eat, drink, love, move about, and wear their jackets; when from these commonplace sentences and pictures they try to draw a moral—a petty moral, easy of comprehension and convenient for domestic use; when in a thousand variations I am offered the same thing over and over again—I run away as Maupassant ran away from the Eiffel Tower which weighed upon his brain with its vulgarity.

SORIN. You can't do without the stage.

TREPLEV. We need new forms of expression. We need new forms, and if we can't have them we had better have nothing (*looks at his watch*). I love my mother—I love her very much—but she leads a senseless sort of life, always taken up with this literary gentleman, her name is always trotted out in the papers—and that wearies me. And sometimes the simple egoism of an ordinary mortal makes me feel sorry that my mother is a celebrated actress, and I fancy that if she were an ordinary woman I should be happier. Uncle, what could be more hopeless and stupid than my position? She used to have visitors, all celebrities—artists and authors—and among them all I was the only one who was nothing, and they only put up with me because I was her son. Who am I? What am I? I left the University in my third year—owing to circumstances "for which we accept no responsibility," as the editors say; I have no talents, I haven't a penny of my own, and on my passport I am described as an artisan of Kiev. You know my father was an artisan of Kiev, though he too was a well-known actor. So, when in her drawing-room all these artists and authors graciously noticed me, I always fancied from their faces that they were taking the measure of my insignificance—I guessed their thoughts and suffered from the humiliation. . . .

SORIN. And, by the way, can you tell me, please, what sort of man this literary gentleman is? There's no making him out. He never says anything.

TREPLEV. He is an intelligent man, good-natured and rather melancholy, you know. A very decent fellow. He is still a good distance off forty, but he is already celebrated and has enough and to spare of everything. As for his writings . . . what shall I say? They are charming, full of talent, but . . . after Tolstoy or Zola you do not care to read Trigorin.

SORIN. Well, I am fond of authors, my boy. At one time I had a passionate desire for two things: I wanted to get married, and I wanted to become an author; but I did not succeed in doing either. Yes, it is pleasant to be even a small author, as a matter of fact.

TREPLEV (*listens*). I hear steps . . . (*embraces his uncle*). I cannot live without her. . . . The very sound of her footsteps is lovely. . . . I am wildly happy (*goes quickly to meet* NINA ZARETCHNY *as she enters*). My enchantress—my dream. . . .

NINA (*in agitation*). I am not late. . . . Of course I am not late. . . .

TREPLEV (*kissing her hands*). No, no, no!

NINA. I have been uneasy all day. I was so frightened. I was afraid father would not let me come. . . . But he has just gone out with my stepmother. The sky is red, the moon is just rising, and I kept urging on the horse (*laughs*). But I am glad (*shakes* SORIN'S *hand warmly*).

SORIN (*laughs*). Your eyes look as though you have been crying. . . . Fie, fie! That's not right!

NINA. Oh, it was nothing. . . . You see how out of breath I am. I have to go in half an hour. We must make haste. I can't stay, I can't! For God's sake don't keep me! My father doesn't know I am here.

TREPLEV. It really is time to begin. We must go and call the others.

SORIN. I'll go this minute (*goes to the right, singing* "To France two grenadiers." *Looks round*) Once I sang like that, and a deputy prosecutor said to me, "You have a powerful voice, your Excellency"; then he thought a little and added, "but not a pleasant one" (*laughs and goes off*).

NINA. My father and his wife won't let me come here. They say it is so Bohemian here . . . they are afraid I shall go on the stage. . . . But I feel drawn to the lake here like a sea-gull. . . . My heart is full of you (*looks round*).

TREPLEV. We are alone.

NINA. I fancy there is someone there.

TREPLEV. There's nobody. (*They kiss.*)

NINA. What tree is this?

TREPLEV. An elm.

NINA. Why is it so dark?

TREPLEV. It's evening; everything is getting dark. Don't go away early, I entreat you!

NINA. I must.

TREPLEV. And if I come to you, Nina, I'll stand in the garden all night, watching your window.

NINA. You can't; the watchman would notice you. Trésor is not used to you, and he would bark.

TREPLEV. I love you!

NINA. Sh-h. . . .

TREPLEV (*hearing footsteps*). Who is there? You, Yakov?

YAKOV (*behind the stage*). Yes, sir.

TREPLEV. Take your places. It's time to begin. Is the moon rising?

YAKOV. Yes, sir.

TREPLEV. Have you got the methylated spirit? Have you got the sulphur? When the red eyes appear there must be a smell of sulphur. (*To* NINA) Go, it's all ready. Are you nervous?

NINA. Yes, awfully! Your mother is all right—I am not afraid of her—but there's Trigorin . . . I feel frightened and ashamed of acting before him . . . a celebrated author. . . . Is he young?

TREPLEV. Yes.

NINA. How wonderful his stories are.

TREPLEV (*coldly*). I don't know. I haven't read them.

NINA. It is difficult to act in your play. There are no living characters in it.

TREPLEV. Living characters! One must depict life not as it is, and not as it ought to be, but as we see it in our dreams.

NINA. There is very little action in your play—nothing but speeches. And to my mind there ought to be love in a play. (*Both go behind the stage.*)

(*Enter* POLINA ANDREYEVNA *and* DORN.)

POLINA. It is getting damp. Go back and put on your goloshes.

DORN. I am hot.

POLINA. You don't take care of yourself. It's obstinacy. You are a doctor, and you know perfectly well that damp air is bad for you, but you want to make me miserable; you sat out on the verandah all yesterday evening on purpose....

DORN (*hums*). "Do not say that youth is ruined."

POLINA. You were so absorbed in conversation with Irina Nikolayevna . . . you did not notice the cold. Own up . . . you are attracted by her.

DORN. I am fifty-five.

POLINA. Nonsense! That's not old for a man. You look very young for your age, and are still attractive to women.

DORN. Well, what would you have?

POLINA. All you men are ready to fall down and worship an actress, all of you!

DORN (*hums*). "Before thee once again I stand." If artists are liked in society and treated differently from merchants, for example, that's only in the nature of things. It's idealism.

POLINA. Women have always fallen in love with you and thrown themselves on your neck. Is that idealism too?

DORN (*shrugs his shoulders*). Well, in the attitude of women to me there has been a great deal that was good. What they principally loved in me was a first-rate doctor. You remember that ten or fifteen years ago I was the only decent accoucheur in the district. Then, too, I have always been an honest man.

POLINA (*seizes him by the hand*). Dearest!

DORN. Sh-h! They are coming.

(*Enter* MADAME ARKADIN *arm in arm with* SORIN, TRIGORIN, SHAMRAEV, MEDVEDENKO *and* MASHA.)

SHAMRAEV. In the year 1873 she acted marvellously at the fair at Poltava. It was a delight! She acted exquisitely! Do you happen to know, madam, where Pavel Semyonitch Tchadin, a comic actor, is now? His Rasplyuev was inimitable, even finer than Sadovsky's, I assure you, honoured lady. Where is he now?

MADAME ARKADIN. You keep asking me about antediluvians. How should I know? (*sits down*).

SHAMRAEV (*with a sigh*). Pashka Tchadin! There are no such actors now. The stage has gone down, Irina Nikolayevna! In old days there were mighty oaks, but now we see nothing but stumps.

DORN. There are few actors of brilliant talents nowadays, that's true; but the average level of acting is far higher than it was.

SHAMRAEV. I can't agree with you. But, of

course, it's a matter of taste. *De gustibus aut bene aut nihil.*

(TREPLEV *comes out from behind the stage.*)

MADAME ARKADIN (*to her son*). My dear son, when is it going to begin ?

TREPLEV. In a minute. I beg you to be patient.

MADAME ARKADIN (*recites from* " Hamlet ").

" Oh, Hamlet, speak no more !
Thou turn'st mine eyes into my very soul ;
And there I see such black and grained spots
As will not leave their tinct."

TREPLEV (*from* " Hamlet ").

" And let me wring your heart, for so I shall,
If it be made of penetrable stuff."

(*A horn is sounded behind the stage.*)

TREPLEV. Ladies and gentlemen, we begin ! I beg you to attend (*a pause*). I begin (*taps with a stick and recites aloud*). Oh, you venerable old shadows that float at night-time over this lake, lull us to sleep and let us dream of what will be in two hundred thousand years !

SORIN. There will be nothing in two hundred thousand years.

TREPLEV. Then let them present that nothing to us.

MADAME ARKADIN. Let them. We are asleep.

(*The curtain rises ; the view of the lake is revealed ; the moon is above the horizon, its reflection in the water ;* NINA ZARETCHNY, *all in white, is sitting on a big stone.*)

NINA. Men, lions, eagles and partridges, horned

deer, geese, spiders, silent fish that dwell in the water, starfishes and creatures which cannot be seen by the eye—all living things, all living things, all living things, having completed their cycle of sorrow, are extinct. . . . For thousands of years the earth has borne no living creature on its surface, and this poor moon lights its lamp in vain. On the meadow the cranes no longer waken with a cry, and there is no sound of the May beetles in the lime trees. It is cold, cold, cold! Empty, empty, empty! Dreadful, dreadful, dreadful! (*a pause*). The bodies of living creatures have vanished into dust, and eternal matter has transformed them into rocks, into water, into clouds, while the souls of all have melted into one. That world-soul I am—I. . . . In me is the soul of Alexander the Great, of Cæsar, of Shakespeare and of Napoleon, and of the lowest leech. In me the consciousness of men is blended with the instincts of the animals, and I remember all, all, all! And I live through every life over again in myself! (*Will-of-the-wisps appear.*)

MADAME ARKADIN (*softly*). It's something decadent.

TREPLEV (*in an imploring and reproachful voice*). Mother!

NINA. I am alone. Once in a hundred years I open my lips to speak, and my voice echoes mournfully in the void, and no one hears. . . . You too, pale lights, hear me no . . . . The stagnant marsh begets you before daybreak and you wander until dawn, but without thought, without will, without the tremor of life. For fear that life should spring up in you the father of eternal matter, the devil, keeps the atoms in you, as in the stones and in the water, in continual flux, and you are changing perpetually. For in all the universe nothing remains permanent and unchanged but the spirit (*a pause*). Like a prisoner cast into a deep, empty well I know not where I am and what awaits me. All is hidden from me but that in the cruel, persistent struggle with the devil—the principle of the forces of matter—I am destined to conquer, and, after that, matter and spirit will be blended in glorious harmony and the Kingdom of the Cosmic Will will come. But that will come only little by little, through long, long thousands of years when the moon and the bright Sirius and the earth are changed to dust. . . . Till then—terror, terror . . . (*a pause; two red spots appear upon the background of the lake*). Here my powerful foe, the devil, is approaching. I see his dreadful crimson eyes. . . .

MADAME ARKADIN. There's a smell of sulphur. Is that as it should be?

TREPLEV. Yes.

MADAME ARKADIN (*laughs*). Oh, it's a stage effect!

TREPLEV. Mother!

NINA. He is dreary without man——

POLINA (*to* DORN). You have taken your hat off. Put it on or you will catch cold.

MADAME ARKADIN. The doctor has taken his hat off to the devil, the father of eternal matter.

TREPLEV (*firing up, aloud*). The play is over! Enough! Curtain!

MADAME ARKADIN. What are you cross about?

TREPLEV. Enough! The curtain! Let down the curtain! (*stamping*). Curtain! (*The curtain falls.*) I am sorry! I lost sight of the fact that only a few of the elect may write plays and act in them. I have infringed the monopoly. I . . . I . . . (*tries to say something more, but with a wave of his hand goes out on left*).

MADAME ARKADIN. What's the matter with him?

SORIN. Irina, you really must have more consideration for youthful vanity, my dear.

MADAME ARKADIN. What did I say to him?

SORIN. You hurt his feelings.

MADAME ARKADIN. He told us beforehand that it was a joke, and I regarded his play as a joke.

SORIN. All the same . . .

MADAME ARKADIN. Now it appears that he has written a great work. What next! So he has got up this performance and smothered us with sulphur not as a joke but as a protest. . . . He wanted to show us how to write and what to act. This is getting tiresome! These continual sallies at my expense—these continual pin-pricks would put anyone out of patience, say what you like. He is a vain, whimsical boy!

SORIN. He meant to give you pleasure.

MADAME ARKADIN. Really? He did not choose an ordinary play, however, but made us listen to this decadent delirium. For the sake of a joke I am ready to listen to delirium, but here we have pretensions to new forms and a new view of art. To my thinking it's no question of new forms at all, but simply bad temper.

TRIGORIN. Everyone writes as he likes and as he can.

MADAME ARKADIN. Let him write as he likes and as he can, only let him leave me in peace.

DORN. Jupiter! you are angry. . . .

MADAME ARKADIN. I am not Jupiter—I am a woman (*lights a cigarette*). I am not angry—I am only vexed that a young man should spend his time so drearily. I did not mean to hurt his feelings.

MEDVEDENKO. No one has any grounds to separate spirit from matter, seeing that spirit itself may be a combination of material atoms. (*With animation, to* TRIGORIN) But you know someone ought to write a play on how we poor teachers live, and get it acted. We have a hard, hard life.

MADAME ARKADIN. That's true, but don't let us talk either of plays or of atoms. It is such a glorious evening! Do you hear? There is singing! (*listens*). How nice it is!

POLINA. It's on the other side of the lake (*a pause*).

MADAME ARKADIN (*to* TRIGORIN). Sit down beside me. Ten or fifteen years ago there were sounds of music and singing on that lake continually almost every night. There are six country houses on the shores of the lake. I remember laughter, noise, shooting, and love affairs without end. . . . The *jeune premier* and the idol of all those six households was in those days our friend here, the doctor (*motions with her head towards* DORN), Yevgeny Sergeitch. He is fascinating still, but in those days he was irresistible. But my conscience is beginning to trouble me. Why did I hurt my poor boy's feelings? I feel worried. (*Aloud*) Kostya! Son! Kostya!

MASHA. I'll go and look for him.

MADAME ARKADIN. Please do, my dear.

MASHA (*going to the left*). Aa-oo! Konstantin Gavrilitch! Aa-oo! (*goes off*).

NINA (*coming out from behind the stage*). Apparently there will be no going on, and I may come out. Good evening! (*kisses* MADAME ARKADIN *and* POLINA ANDREYEVNA).

SORIN. Bravo! Bravo!

MADAME ARKADIN. Bravo! Bravo! We admired you. With such an appearance, with such a lovely voice, you really cannot stay in the country; it is a sin. You must have talent. Do you hear? It's your duty to go on the stage.

NINA. Oh, that's my dream! (*sighing*). But it will never be realised.

MADAME ARKADIN. Who knows? Here, let me introduce Boris Alexeyevitch Trigorin.

NINA. Oh, I am so glad . . . (*overcome with embarrassment*). I am always reading your . . .

MADAME ARKADIN (*making her sit down beside them*). Don't be shy, my dear. He is a celebrity, but he has a simple heart. You see, he is shy himself.

DORN. I suppose we may raise the curtain; it's rather uncanny.

SHAMRAEV (*aloud*). Yakov, pull up the curtain, my lad. (*The curtain goes up.*)

NINA (*to* TRIGORIN). It is a queer play, isn't it?

TRIGORIN. I did not understand it at all. But I enjoyed it. You acted so genuinely. And the scenery was delightful (*a pause*). There must be a lot of fish in that lake.

NINA. Yes.

TRIGORIN. I love angling. There is nothing I enjoy so much as sitting on the bank of a river in the evening and watching the float.

NINA. But I should have thought that for anyone who has known the enjoyment of creation, no other enjoyment can exist.

MADAME ARKADIN (*laughing*). Don't talk like that. When people say nice things to him he is utterly floored.

SHAMRAEV. I remember one evening in the opera theatre in Moscow the celebrated Silva took the lower *C* ! As it happened, there was sitting in the gallery the bass of our church choir, and all at once—imagine our intense astonishment—we heard from the gallery " Bravo, Silva ! " a whole octave lower—like this : (*in a deep bass*) " Bravo, Silva ! " The audience sat spellbound (*a pause*).

DORN. The angel of silence has flown over us.

NINA. It's time for me to go. Good-bye.

MADAME ARKADIN. Where are you off to ? Why so early ? We won't let you go.

NINA. My father expects me.

MADAME ARKADIN. What a man, really . . . (*kisses her*). Well, there is no help for it. I am sorry—I am sorry to let you go.

NINA. If you knew how grieved I am to go.

MADAME ARKADIN. Someone ought to see you home, my little dear.

NINA (*frightened*). Oh, no, no!

SORIN (*to her, in an imploring voice*). Do stay!

NINA. I can't, Pyotr Nikolayevitch.

SORIN. Stay for an hour. What is there in that?

NINA (*thinking a minute, tearfully*). I can't! (*shakes hands and hurriedly goes off*).

MADAME ARKADIN. Unfortunate girl she is, really. They say her mother left her father all her immense property—every farthing of it—and now the girl has got nothing, as her father has already made a will leaving everything to his second wife. It's monstrous!

DORN. Yes, her father is a pretty thorough scoundrel, one must do him the justice to say so.

SORIN (*rubbing his cold hands*). Let us go too, it's getting damp. My legs ache.

MADAME ARKADIN. They seem like wooden legs, you can hardly walk. Let us go, unlucky old man! (*takes his arm*).

SHAMRAEV (*offering his arm to his wife*). Madame?

SORIN. I hear that dog howling again. (*To* SHAMRAEV) Be so kind, Ilya Afanasyitch, as to tell them to let it off the chain.

SHAMRAEV. It's impossible, Pyotr Nikolayevitch, I am afraid of thieves getting into the barn. Our millet is there. (*To* MEDVEDENKO *who is walking beside him*) Yes, a whole octave lower: "Bravo, Silva!" And he not a singer—simply a church chorister!

MEDVEDENKO. And what salary does a chorister get? (*All go out except* DORN.)

DORN (*alone*). I don't know, perhaps I know nothing about it, or have gone off my head, but

I liked the play. There is something in it. When that girl talked about loneliness and afterwards when the devil's eyes appeared, I was so excited that my hands trembled. It is fresh, naïve. . . . Here he comes, I believe. I want to say all the nice things I can to him.

TREPLEV (*enters*). They have all gone.

DORN. I am here.

TREPLEV. Mashenka is looking for me all over the park. Insufferable creature she is!

DORN. Konstantin Gavrilitch, I liked your play extremely. It's a strange thing, and I haven't heard the end, and yet it made a strong impression! You are a gifted man—you must persevere.

(TREPLEV *presses his hand warmly and embraces him impulsively.*)

DORN. Fie, what an hysterical fellow! There are tears in his eyes! What I mean is this. You have taken a subject from the realm of abstract ideas. So it should be, for a work of art ought to express a great idea. A thing is only fine when it is serious. How pale you are!

TREPLEV. So you tell me to persevere?

DORN. Yes. . . . But write only of what is important and eternal. You know, I have had varied experiences of life, and have enjoyed it; I am satisfied, but if it had been my lot to know the spiritual heights which artists reach at the moment of creation, I should, I believe, have despised my bodily self and all that appertains to it and left all things earthly as far behind as possible.

TREPLEV. Excuse me, where is Nina?

DORN. And another thing. In a work of art

there ought to be a clear definite idea. You ought to know what is your aim in writing, for if you go along that picturesque route without a definite goal you will be lost and your talent will be your ruin.

TREPLEV (*impatiently*). Where is Nina?

DORN. She has gone home.

TREPLEV (*in despair*). What am I to do? I want to see her . . . I must see her. . . . I must go. . . .

(*Enter* MASHA.)

DORN (*to* TREPLEV). Calm yourself, my boy.

TREPLEV. But I am going all the same. I must go.

MASHA. Come indoors, Konstantin Gavrilitch. Your mother wants you. She is worried.

TREPLEV. Tell her that I have gone away. And I beg you—all of you—leave me in peace! Let me alone! Don't follow me about!

DORN. Come, come, come, dear boy. . . . You can't go on like that. . . . That's not the thing.

TREPLEV (*in tears*). Good-bye, doctor. Thank you . . . (*goes off*).

DORN (*with a sigh*). Youth! youth!

MASHA. When people have nothing better to say, they say, "Youth! youth!" . . . (*takes a pinch of snuff*).

DORN (*takes her snuff-box from her and flings it into the bushes*). That's disgusting! (*a pause*). I believe they are playing the piano indoors. We must go in.

MASHA. Wait a little.

DORN. What is it?

MASHA. I want to tell you once more. I have a longing to talk . . . (*growing agitated*). I don't care for my father . . . but I feel drawn to you. For some reason I feel with all my heart that you are very near me. . . . Help me. Help me, or I shall do something silly, I shall make a mock of my life and ruin it. . . . I can't go on. . . .

DORN. What is it ? Help you in what ?

MASHA. I am miserable. No one, no one knows how miserable I am ! (*Laying her head on his breast, softly*) I love Konstantin !

DORN. How hysterical they all are ! How hysterical ! And what a lot of love. . . . Oh, the sorcery of the lake ! (*Tenderly*) But what can I do, my child ? What ? What ?

CURTAIN.

ACT II

A croquet lawn. The house with a big verandah in the background on the right, on the left is seen the lake with the blazing sun reflected in it. Flower beds. Midday. Hot. MADAME ARKADIN, DORN *and* MASHA *are sitting on a garden seat in the shade of an old lime tree on one side of the croquet lawn.* DORN *has an open book on his knee.*

MADAME ARKADIN (*to* MASHA). Come, let us stand up. (*They both get up.*) Let us stand side by side. You are twenty-two and I am nearly twice as old. Yevgeny Sergeitch, which of us looks the younger?

DORN. You, of course.

MADAME ARKADIN. There! And why is it? Because I work, I feel I am always on the go, while you stay always in the same place and have no life at all. . . . And it is my rule never to look into the future. I never think about old age or death. What is to be, will be.

MASHA. And I feel as though I had been born long, long ago; I trail my life along like an endless train. . . . And often I have not the slightest desire to go on living (*sits down*). Of course, that's all nonsense. I must shake myself and throw it all off.

DORN (*hums quietly*). "Tell her, my flowers."

MADAME ARKADIN. Then I am as particular as an Englishman. I keep myself in hand, as they say, my dear, and am always dressed and have my hair done *comme il faut.* Do I allow myself to go out of the house even into the garden in a dressing-gown, or without my hair being done? Never! What has preserved me, is that I have never been a dowdy, I have never let myself go, as some women do . . . (*walks about the lawn with her arms akimbo*). Here I am, as brisk as a bird. I could take the part of a girl of fifteen.

DORN. Nevertheless, I shall go on (*takes up the book*). We stopped at the corn merchant and the rats. . . .

MADAME ARKADIN. And the rats. Read (*sits down*). But give it to me, I'll read. It is my turn (*takes the book and looks in it*). And rats. . . . Here it is. . . . (*Reads*) "And of course for society people to spoil novelists and to attract them to themselves is as dangerous as for a corn merchant to rear rats in his granaries. And yet they love them. And so, when a woman has picked out an author whom she desires to captivate, she lays siege to him by means of compliments, flattery and favours . . ." Well, that may be so with the French, but there is nothing like that with us, we have no set rules. Among us, before a woman sets to work to captivate an author, she is generally head over ears in love herself, if you please. To go no further, take Trigorin and me. . . .

(*Enter* SORIN, *leaning on his stick and with him* NINA; MEDVEDENKO *wheels an empty bath-chair in after them.*)

SORIN (*in a caressing tone, as to a child*). Yes? We are delighted, aren't we? We are happy to-day at last? (*To his sister*) We are delighted! Our father and stepmother have gone off to Tver, and we are free now for three whole days.

NINA (*sits down beside* MADAME ARKADIN *and embraces her*). I am happy! Now I belong to you.

SORIN (*sits down in his bath-chair*). She looks quite a beauty to-day.

MADAME ARKADIN. Nicely dressed and interesting. . . . That's a good girl (*kisses* NINA). But we mustn't praise you too much for fear of ill-luck. Where is Boris Alexeyevitch?

NINA. He is in the bathing-house, fishing.

MADAME ARKADIN. I wonder he doesn't get sick of it! (*is about to go on reading*).

NINA. What is that?

MADAME ARKADIN. Maupassant's "Sur l'eau," my dear (*reads a few lines to herself*). Well, the rest isn't interesting or true (*shuts the book*). I feel uneasy. Tell me, what's wrong with my son? Why is he so depressed and ill-humoured? He spends whole days on the lake and I hardly ever see him.

MASHA. His heart is troubled. (*To* NINA, *timidly*) Please, do read us something out of his play!

NINA (*shrugging her shoulders*). Would you like it? It's so uninteresting.

MASHA (*restraining her enthusiasm*). When he

reads anything himself his eyes glow and his face turns pale. He has a fine mournful voice, and the gestures of a poet.

(*There is a sound of* SORIN *snoring.*)

DORN. Good-night!

MADAME ARKADIN. Petrusha!

SORIN. Ah?

MADAME ARKADIN. Are you asleep?

SORIN. Not a bit of it (*a pause*).

MADAME ARKADIN. You do nothing for your health, brother, and that's not right.

SORIN. I should like to take something, but the doctor won't give me anything.

DORN. Take medicine at sixty!

SORIN. Even at sixty one wants to live!

DORN (*with vexation*). Oh, very well, take valerian drops!

MADAME ARKADIN. It seems to me it would do him good to go to some mineral springs.

DORN. Well, he might go. And he might not.

MADAME ARKADIN. What is one to make of that?

DORN. There's nothing to make of it. It's quite clear (*a pause*).

MEDVEDENKO. Pyotr Nikolayevitch ought to give up smoking.

SORIN. Nonsense!

DORN. No, it's not nonsense. Wine and tobacco destroy the personality. After a cigar or a glass of vodka, you are not Pyotr Nikolayevitch any more but Pyotr Nikolayevitch plus somebody else; your ego is diffused and you feel towards yourself as to a third person.

SORIN (*laughs*). It's all very well for you to argue! You've lived your life, but what about me? I have served in the Department of Justice for twenty-eight years, but I haven't lived yet, I've seen and done nothing as a matter of fact, and very naturally I want to live very much. You've had enough and you don't care, and so you are inclined to be philosophical, but I want to live, and so I drink sherry at dinner and smoke cigars and so on. That's all it comes to.

DORN. One must look at life seriously, but to go in for cures at sixty and to regret that one hasn't enjoyed oneself enough in one's youth is frivolous, if you will forgive my saying so.

MASHA (*gets up*). It must be lunch-time (*walks with a lazy, lagging step*). My leg is gone to sleep (*goes off*).

DORN. She will go and have a couple of glasses before lunch.

SORIN. She has no personal happiness, poor thing.

DORN. Nonsense, your Excellency.

SORIN. You argue like a man who has had all he wants.

MADAME ARKADIN. Oh, what can be more boring than this sweet country boredom! Hot, still, no one ever doing anything, everyone airing their theories. . . . It's nice being with you, my friends, charming to listen to you, but . . . to sit in a hotel room somewhere and learn one's part is ever so much better.

NINA (*enthusiastically*). Delightful! I understand you.

SORIN. Of course, it's better in town. You sit in your study, the footman lets no one in unannounced, there's a telephone . . . in the streets there are cabs and everything. . . .

DORN (*hums*). "Tell her, my flowers."

(*Enter* SHAMRAEV, *and after him* POLINA ANDREYEVNA.)

SHAMRAEV. Here they are! Good morning! (*kisses* MADAME ARKADIN'S *hand and then* NINA'S). Delighted to see you in good health. (*To* MADAME ARKADIN) My wife tells me that you are proposing to drive into town with her to-day. Is that so?

MADAME ARKADIN. Yes, we are thinking of it.

SHAMRAEV. Hm! that's splendid, but how are you going, honoured lady? They are carting the rye to-day; all the men are at work. What horses are you to have, allow me to ask?

MADAME ARKADIN. What horses? How can I tell which?

SORIN. We've got carriage horses.

SHAMRAEV (*growing excited*). Carriage horses! But where am I to get collars for them? Where am I to get collars? It's a strange thing! It passes my understanding! Honoured lady! forgive me, I am full of reverence for your talent. I would give ten years of my life for you, but I cannot let you have the horses!

MADAME ARKADIN. But if I have to go! It's a queer thing!

SHAMRAEV. Honoured lady! you don't know what farming means.

MADAME ARKADIN (*flaring up*). That's the old story! If that's so, I go back to Moscow to-day.

Give orders for horses to be hired for me at the village, or I'll walk to the station.

SHAMRAEV (*flaring up*). In that case I resign my position! You must look for another steward (*goes off*).

MADAME ARKADIN. It's like this every summer; every summer I am insulted here! I won't set my foot in the place again (*goes off at left where the bathing shed is supposed to be; a minute later she can be seen entering the house.* TRIGORIN *follows her, carrying fishing rods and tackle, and a pail*).

SORIN (*flaring up*). This is insolence! It's beyond everything. I am thoroughly sick of it. Send all the horses here this minute!

NINA (*to* POLINA ANDREYEVNA). To refuse Irina Nikolayevna, the famous actress! Any wish of hers, any whim even, is of more consequence than all your farming. It's positively incredible!

POLINA (*in despair*). What can I do? Put yourself in my position: what can I do?

SORIN (*to* NINA). Let us go to my sister. We will all entreat her not to go away. Won't we? (*Looking in the direction in which* SHAMRAEV *has gone*) Insufferable man! Despot!

NINA (*preventing him from getting up*). Sit still, sit still. We will wheel you in. (*She and* MEDVEDENKO *push the bath-chair.*) Oh, how awful it is!

SORIN. Yes, yes, it's awful. But he won't leave, I'll speak to him directly. (*They go out;* DORN *and* POLINA ANDREYEVNA *are left alone on the stage.*)

DORN. People are tiresome. Your husband ought to be simply kicked out, but it will end in that old woman Pyotr Nikolayevitch and his sister begging the man's pardon. You will see!

POLINA. He has sent the carriage horses into the fields too! And there are misunderstandings like this every day. If you only knew how it upsets me! It makes me ill; see how I am trembling . . . . I can't endure his rudeness. (*In an imploring voice*) Yevgeny, dearest, light of my eyes, my darling, let me come to you. . . . Our time is passing, we are no longer young, and if only we could lay aside concealment and lying for the end of our lives, anyway . . . (*a pause*).

DORN. I am fifty-five; it's too late to change my life.

POLINA. I know you refuse me because there are other women too who are as near to you. You can't take them all to live with you. I understand. Forgive me, you are tired of me.

(NINA *appears near the house; she is picking flowers.*)

DORN. No, it's all right.

POLINA. I am wretched from jealousy. Of course you are a doctor, you can't avoid women. I understand.

DORN (*to* NINA, *who comes up to them*). How are things going?

NINA. Irina Nikolayevna is crying and Pyotr Nikolayevitch has an attack of asthma.

DORN (*gets up*). I'd better go and give them both valerian drops.

NINA (*gives him the flowers*). Please take these

DORN. *Merci bien (goes towards the house).*

POLINA (*going with him*). What charming flowers! (*Near the house, in a smothered voice*) Give me those flowers! Give me those flowers! (*on receiving them tears the flowers to pieces and throws them away; both go into the house*).

NINA (*alone*). How strange it is to see a famous actress cry, and about such a trivial thing! And isn't it strange? A famous author, adored by the public, written about in all the papers, his photographs for sale, his works translated into foreign languages—and he spends the whole day fishing and is delighted that he has caught two gudgeon. I thought famous people were proud, unapproachable, that they despised the crowd, and by their fame and the glory of their name, as it were, revenged themselves on the vulgar herd for putting rank and wealth above everything. But here they cry and fish, play cards, laugh and get cross like everyone else!

TREPLEV (*comes in without a hat on, with a gun and a dead sea-gull*). Are you alone here?

NINA. Yes.

(TREPLEV *lays the sea-gull at her feet.*)

NINA. What does that mean?

TREPLEV. I was so mean as to kill this bird to-day. I lay it at your feet.

NINA. What is the matter with you? (*picks up the bird and looks at it*).

TREPLEV (*after a pause*). Soon I shall kill myself in the same way.

NINA. You have so changed, I hardly know you.

TREPLEV. Yes, ever since the day when I hardly

knew you. You have changed to me, your eyes are cold, you feel me in the way.

NINA. You have become irritable of late, you express yourself so incomprehensibly, as it were in symbols. This bird is a symbol too, I suppose, but forgive me, I don't understand it (*lays the sea-gull on the seat*). I am too simple to understand you.

TREPLEV. This began from that evening when my play came to grief so stupidly. Women never forgive failure. I have burnt it all; every scrap of it. If only you knew how miserable I am! Your growing cold to me is awful, incredible, as though I had woken up and found this lake had suddenly dried up or sunk into the earth. You have just said that you are too simple to understand me. Oh, what is there to understand? My play was not liked, you despise my inspiration, you already consider me commonplace, insignificant, like so many others . . . (*stamping*). How well I understand it all, how I understand it! I feel as though I had a nail in my brain, damnation take it together with my vanity which is sucking away my life, sucking it like a snake . . . (*sees* TRIGORIN, *who comes in reading a book*). Here comes the real genius, walking like Hamlet and with a book too. (*Mimics*) "Words, words, words." . . . The sun has scarcely reached you and you are smiling already, your eyes are melting in its rays. I won't be in your way (*goes off quickly*).

TRIGORIN (*making notes in his book*). Takes snuff and drinks vodka. Always in black. The schoolmaster is in love with her. . . .

Nina. Good morning, Boris Alexeyevitch!

Trigorin. Good morning. Circumstances have turned out so unexpectedly that it seems we are setting off to-day. We are hardly likely to meet again. I am sorry. I don't often have the chance of meeting young girls, youthful and charming; I have forgotten how one feels at eighteen or nineteen and can't picture it to myself, and so the young girls in my stories and novels are usually false. I should like to be in your shoes just for one hour to find out how you think, and altogether what sort of person you are.

Nina. And I should like to be in your shoes.

Trigorin. What for?

Nina. To know what it feels like to be a famous, gifted author. What does it feel like to be famous? How does it affect you, being famous?

Trigorin. How? Nohow, I believe. I have never thought about it. (*After a moment's thought*) It's one of two things: either you exaggerate my fame, or it never is felt at all.

Nina. But if you read about yourself in the newspapers?

Trigorin. When they praise me I am pleased, and when they abuse me I feel out of humour for a day or two.

Nina. What a wonderful world! If only you knew how I envy you! How different people's lots in life are! Some can scarcely get through their dull, obscure existence, they are all just like one another, they are all unhappy; while others —you, for instance—you are one out of a million, have an interesting life full of brightness and significance. You are happy.

TRIGORIN. I? (*shrugging his shoulders*). Hm. . . . You talk of fame and happiness, of bright interesting life, but to me all those fine words, if you will forgive my saying so, are just like a sweetmeat which I never taste. You are very young and very good-natured.

NINA. Your life is splendid!

TRIGORIN. What is there particularly nice in it? (*Looks at his watch*) I must go and write directly. Excuse me, I mustn't stay . . . (*laughs*). You have stepped on my favourite corn, as the saying is, and here I am beginning to get excited and a little cross. Let us talk though. We will talk about my splendid bright life. . . . Well, where shall we begin? (*After thinking a little*) There are such things as fixed ideas, when a man thinks day and night for instance, of nothing but the moon. And I have just such a moon. I am haunted day and night by one persistent thought: I ought to be writing, I ought to be writing, I ought . . . I have scarcely finished one novel when, for some reason, I must begin writing another, then a third, after the third a fourth. I write incessantly, post haste, and I can't write in any other way. What is there splendid and bright in that, I ask you? Oh, it's an absurd life! Here I am with you; I am excited, yet every moment I remember that my unfinished novel is waiting for me. Here I see a cloud that looks like a grand piano. I think that I must put into a story somewhere that a cloud sailed by that looked like a grand piano. There is a scent of heliotrope. I hurriedly make a note: a sickly smell, a widow's flower, to be mentioned in the description of a summer evening. I catch up myself and you at every sentence, every word, and make haste to put those sentences and words away into my literary treasure-house—it may come in useful! When I finish work I race off to the theatre or to fishing; if only I could rest in that and forget myself. But no, there's a new subject rolling about in my head like a heavy iron cannon ball, and I am drawn to my writing table and must make haste again to go on writing and writing. And it's always like that, always. And I have no rest from myself, and I feel that I am eating up my own life, and that for the sake of the honey I give to someone in space I am stripping the pollen from my best flowers, tearing up the flowers themselves and trampling on their roots. Don't you think I am mad? Do my friends and acquaintances treat me as though I were sane? "What are you writing? What are you giving us?" It's the same thing again and again, and it seems to me as though my friends' notice, their praises, their enthusiasm—that it's all a sham, that they are deceiving me as an invalid and I am somehow afraid that they will steal up to me from behind, snatch me and carry me off and put me in a mad-house. And in those years, the best years of my youth, when I was beginning, my writing was unmixed torture. A small writer, particularly when he is not successful, seems to himself clumsy, awkward, unnecessary; his nerves are strained and overwrought. He can't resist hanging about people connected with literature and art, unrecognised and unnoticed by anyone, afraid to look anyone boldly in the face, like a passionate gambler without any money. I hadn't seen my reader, but for some reason I always imagined him hostile, and mistrustful. I was afraid of the public, it alarmed me, and when I had to produce my first play it always seemed to me that all the dark people felt hostile and all the fair ones were coldly indifferent. Oh, how awful it was! What agony it was!

NINA. But surely inspiration and the very process of creation give you moments of exalted happiness?

TRIGORIN. Yes. While I am writing I enjoy it. And I like reading my proofs, but . . . as soon as it is published I can't endure it, and I see that it is all wrong, a mistake, that it ought not to have been written at all, and I feel vexed and sick about it . . . (*laughing*). And the public reads it and says: "Yes, charming, clever. Charming, but very inferior to Tolstoy," or, "It's a fine thing, but Turgenev's 'Fathers and Children' is finer." And it will be the same to my dying day, only charming and clever, charming and clever—and nothing more. And when I die my friends, passing by my tomb, will say, "Here lies Trigorin. He was a good writer, but inferior to Turgenev."

NINA. Forgive me, but I refuse to understand you. You are simply spoiled by success.

TRIGORIN. What success? I have never liked

myself; I dislike my own work. The worst of it is that I am in a sort of delirium, and often don't understand what I am writing. I love this water here, the trees, the sky. I feel nature, it arouses in me a passionate, irresistible desire to write. But I am not simply a landscape painter; I am also a citizen. I love my native country, my people; I feel that if I am a writer I am in duty bound to write of the people, of their sufferings, of their future, to talk about science and the rights of man and so on, and so on, and I write about everything. I am hurried and flustered, and on all sides they whip me up and are angry with me; I dash about from side to side like a fox beset by hounds. I see life and culture continually getting farther and farther away while I fall farther and farther behind like a peasant too late for the train; and what it comes to is that I feel I can only describe scenes and in everything else I am false to the marrow of my bones.

NINA. You are overworked and have not the leisure nor the desire to appreciate your own significance. You may be dissatisfied with yourself, but for others you are great and splendid! If I were a writer like you, I should give up my whole life to the common herd, but I should know that there could be no greater happiness for them than to rise to my level, and they would harness themselves to my chariot.

TRIGORIN. My chariot, what next! Am I an Agamemnon, or what? (*Both smile.*)

NINA. For such happiness as being a writer or an artist I would be ready to endure poverty, disappointment, the dislike of those around me; I would live in a garret and eat nothing but rye bread, I would suffer from being dissatisfied with myself, from recognising my own imperfections, but I should ask in return for fame . . . real, resounding fame. . . . (*covers her face with her hands*). It makes me dizzy. . . . Ough!

(*The voice of* MADAME ARKADIN *from the house.*)

MADAME ARKADIN. Boris Alexeyevitch!

TRIGORIN. They are calling for me. I suppose it's to pack. But I don't want to leave here. (*Looks round at the lake*) Just look how glorious it is! It's splendid!

NINA. Do you see the house and garden on the other side of the lake?

TRIGORIN. Yes.

NINA. That house was my dear mother's. I was born there. I have spent all my life beside this lake and I know every little islet on it.

TRIGORIN. It's very delightful here! (*Seeing the sea-gull*) And what's this?

NINA. A sea-gull. Konstantin Gavrilitch shot it.

TRIGORIN. A beautiful bird. Really, I don't want to go away. Try and persuade Irina Nikolayevna to stay (*makes a note in his book*).

NINA. What are you writing?

TRIGORIN. Oh, I am only making a note. A subject struck me (*putting away the note-book*). A subject for a short story: a young girl, such as you, has lived all her life beside a lake; she loves the lake like a sea-gull, and is as free and happy as a sea-gull. But a man comes by chance, sees her, and having nothing better to do, destroys her like that sea-gull here (*a pause*).

(MADAME ARKADIN *appears at the window*.)

MADAME ARKADIN. Boris Alexeyevitch, where are you?

TRIGORIN. I am coming (*goes and looks back at* NINA. *To* MADAME ARKADIN *at the window*) What is it?

MADAME ARKADIN. We are staying.

(TRIGORIN *goes into the house*.)

NINA (*advances to the footlights; after a few moments' meditation*) It's a dream!

CURTAIN.

ACT III

The dining-room in SORIN'S *house. Doors on right and on left. A sideboard. A medicine cupboard. A table in the middle of the room. A portmanteau and hat-boxes; signs of preparation for departure.* TRIGORIN *is having lunch;* MASHA *stands by the table.*

MASHA. I tell all this to you as a writer. You may make use of it. I am telling you the truth: if he had hurt himself seriously I would not have gone on living another minute. But I have pluck enough all the same. I just made up my mind that I would tear this love out of my heart, tear it out by the roots.

TRIGORIN. How are you going to do that?

MASHA. I am going to be married. To Medvedenko.

TRIGORIN. That's the schoolmaster?

MASHA. Yes.

TRIGORIN. I don't understand what's the object of it.

MASHA. To love without hope, to spend whole years waiting for something. . . . But when I marry, there will be no time left for love, new cares will smother all the old feelings. And, anyway, it will be a change, you know. Shall we have another ?

TRIGORIN. Won't that be too much ?

MASHA. Oh, come ! (*fills two glasses*). Don't look at me like that ! Women drink much oftener than you imagine. Only a small proportion drink openly as I do, the majority drink in secret. Yes. And it's always vodka or brandy. (*Clinks glasses*) My best wishes ! You are a good-hearted man ; I am sorry to be parting from you. (*They drink.*)

TRIGORIN. I don't want to go myself.

MASHA. You should beg her to stay.

TRIGORIN. No, she won't stay now. Her son is behaving very tactlessly. First he shoots himself, and now they say he is going to challenge me to a duel. And whatever for ? He sulks, and snorts, and preaches new forms of art. . . . But there is room for all—new and old—why quarrel about it ?

MASHA. Well, there's jealousy too. But it is nothing to do with me.

(*A pause.* YAKOV *crosses from right to left with a portmanteau.* NINA *enters and stands by the window.*)

MASHA. My schoolmaster is not very brilliant, but he is a good-natured man, and poor, and he is very much in love with me. I am sorry for him. And I am sorry for his old mother. Well, let me wish you all happiness. Don't remember evil against me (*shakes hands with him warmly*). I am very grateful for your friendly interest. Send me your books and be sure to put in an inscription. Only don't write, " To my honoured friend," but write simply, " To Marya who belongs nowhere and has no object in life." Good-bye! (*goes out*).

NINA (*stretching out her arm towards* TRIGORIN, *with her fist clenched*). Odd or even?

TRIGORIN. Even.

NINA (*with a sigh*). Wrong. I had only one pea in my hand. I was trying my fortune whether to go on the stage or not. I wish someone would advise me.

TRIGORIN. It's impossible to advise in such a matter (*a pause*).

NINA. We are parting and . . . perhaps we shall never meet again. Won't you please take this little medallion as a parting gift? I had your initials engraved on one side of it . . . and on the other the title of your book, "Days and Nights."

TRIGORIN. How exquisite! (*kisses the medallion*). A charming present!

NINA. Think of me sometimes.

TRIGORIN. I shall think of you. I shall think of you as you were on that sunny day—do you remember?—a week ago, when you were wearing a light dress . . . we were talking . . . there was a white sea-gull lying on the seat.

NINA (*pensively*). Yes, a sea-gull . . . (*a pause*). We can't talk any more, there's someone coming. . . . Let me have two minutes before you go, I entreat you . . . (*goes out on the left*).

(*At the same instant* MADAME ARKADIN, SORIN *in a dress coat with a star of some order on it, then* YAKOV, *occupied with the luggage, enter on the right.*)

MADAME ARKADIN. Stay at home, old man. With your rheumatism you ought not to go gadding about. (*To* TRIGORIN) Who was that went out? Nina?

TRIGORIN. Yes.

MADAME ARKADIN. *Pardon*, we interrupted you (*sits down*). I believe I have packed everything. I am worn out.

TRIGORIN (*reads on the medallion*). "'Days and Nights,' page 121, lines 11 and 12."

YAKOV (*clearing the table*). Am I to pack your fishing things too, sir?

TRIGORIN. Yes, I shall want them again. You can give away the hooks.

YAKOV. Yes, sir.

TRIGORIN (*to himself*). Page 121, lines 11 and 12. What is there in those lines? (*To* MADAME ARKADIN) Are there copies of my books in the house?

MADAME ARKADIN. Yes, in my brother's study, in the corner bookcase.

TRIGORIN. Page 121 . . . (*goes out*).

MADAME ARKADIN. Really, Petrusha, you had better stay at home.

SORIN. You are going away; it will be dreary for me at home without you.

MADAME ARKADIN. And what is there in the town?

SORIN. Nothing particular, but still . . . (*laughs*). There will be the laying of the foundation-stone of the Zemstvo hall, and all that sort of thing. One longs to shake oneself free from this stagnant existence, if only for an hour or two. I've been too long on the shelf like some old cigarette-holder. I have ordered the horses for one o'clock; we'll set off at the same time.

MADAME ARKADIN (*after a pause*). Come, stay here, don't be bored and don't catch cold. Look after my son. Take care of him. Give him good advice (*a pause*). Here I am going away and I shall never know why Konstantin tried to shoot himself. I fancy jealousy was the chief cause, and the sooner I get Trigorin away from here, the better.

SORIN. What can I say? There were other reasons too. It's easy to understand; he is young, intelligent, living in the country, in the wilds, with no money, no position and no future. He has nothing to do. He is ashamed of his idleness and afraid of it. I am very fond of him indeed, and he is attached to me, yet in spite of it all he feels he is superfluous in the house, that he is a dependant, a poor relation. It's easy to understand, it's *amour propre*. . . .

MADAME ARKADIN. He is a great anxiety to me! (*Pondering*) He might go into the service, perhaps.

SORIN (*begins to whistle, then irresolutely*). I think that quite the best thing would be if you were to . . . let him have a little money. In the first place he ought to be able to be dressed like other people and all that. Just look at him, he's been going about in the same wretched jacket for the last three years and he has no overcoat . . . (*laughs*). It would do him no harm to have a little fun . . . to go abroad or something. . . . It wouldn't cost much.

MADAME ARKADIN. But all the same . . . I might manage the suit, perhaps, but as for going abroad . . . No, just at the moment I can't even manage the suit. (*Resolutely*) I have no money!

(SORIN *laughs.*)

MADAME ARKADIN. No!

SORIN (*begins to whistle*). Quite so. Forgive me, my dear, don't be cross. I believe you. . . . You are a generous, noble-hearted woman.

MADAME ARKADIN (*weeping*). I have no money.

SORIN. If I had money, of course I would give him some myself, but I have nothing, not a halfpenny (*laughs*). My steward takes all my pension and spends it all on the land and the cattle and the bees, and my money is all wasted. The bees die, and the cows die, they never let me have horses. . . .

MADAME ARKADIN. Yes, I have money, but you see I am an actress; my dresses alone are enough to ruin me.

SORIN. You are a kind, good creature . . . I respect you. . . . Yes . . . but there, I got a touch of it again . . . (*staggers*). I feel dizzy (*clutches at the table*). I feel ill and all that.

MADAME ARKADIN (*alarmed*). Petrusha! (*trying to support him*). Petrusha, my dear! (*Calling*) Help! help!

(*Enter* TREPLEV *with a bandage round his head and* MEDVEDENKO.)

MADAME ARKADIN. He feels faint!

SORIN. It's all right, it's all right! (*smiles and drinks some water*). It's passed off . . . and all that.

TREPLEV (*to his mother*). Don't be frightened, mother, it's not serious. Uncle often has these attacks now. (*To his uncle*) You must lie down, uncle.

SORIN. For a little while, yes. . . . But I am going to the town all the same. . . . I'll lie down a little and then set off. . . . It's quite natural (*goes out leaning on his stick*).

MEDVEDENKO (*gives him his arm*). There's a riddle: in the morning on four legs, at noon on two, in the evening on three. . . .

SORIN (*laughs*). Just so. And at night on the back. Thank you, I can manage alone. . . .

MEDVEDENKO. Oh come, why stand on ceremony! (*goes out with* SORIN).

MADAME ARKADIN. How he frightened me!

TREPLEV. It is not good for him to live in the country. He gets depressed. If you would be generous for once, mother, and lend him fifteen hundred or two thousand roubles, he could spend a whole year in town.

MADAME ARKADIN. I have no money. I am an actress, not a banker (*a pause*).

TREPLEV. Mother, change my bandage. You do it so well.

MADAME ARKADIN (*takes out of the medicine cupboard some iodoform and a box with bandaging material*). The doctor is late.

TREPLEV. He promised to be here at ten, and it is midday already.

MADAME ARKADIN. Sit down (*takes the band-*

age off his head). It's like a turban. Yesterday a stranger asked in the kitchen what nationality you were. But you have almost completely healed. There is the merest trifle left (*kisses him on the head*). You won't do anything naughty again while I am away, will you?

TREPLEV. No, mother. It was a moment of mad despair when I could not control myself. It won't happen again. (*Kisses her hand*) You have such clever hands. I remember, long ago, when you were still acting at the Imperial Theatre —I was little then—there was a fight in our yard and a washerwoman, one of the tenants, was badly beaten. Do you remember? She was picked up senseless . . . you looked after her, took her remedies and washed her children in a tub. Don't you remember?

MADAME ARKADIN. No (*puts on a fresh bandage*).

TREPLEV. Two ballet dancers lived in the same house as we did at the time. . . . They used to come to you and have coffee. . . .

MADAME ARKADIN. I remember that.

TREPLEV. They were very pious (*a pause*). Just lately, these last days, I have loved you as tenderly and completely as when I was a child. I have no one left now but you. Only why, why do you give yourself up to the influence of that man?

MADAME ARKADIN. You don't understand him, Konstantin. He is a very noble character. . . .

TREPLEV. And yet when he was told I was going to challenge him, the nobility of his character did not prevent him from funking it. He is going away. Ignominious flight!

MADAME ARKADIN. What nonsense! It is I who am asking him to go.

TREPLEV. A very noble character! Here you and I are almost quarrelling over him, and at this very moment he is somewhere in the drawing-room or the garden laughing at us . . . developing Nina, trying to convince her finally that he is a genius.

MADAME ARKADIN. You take a pleasure in saying unpleasant things to me. I respect that man and beg you not to speak ill of him before me,

TREPLEV. And I don't respect him. You want me to think him a genius too, but forgive me, I can't tell lies, his books make me sick.

MADAME ARKADIN. That's envy. There's nothing left for people who have pretension without talent but to attack real talent. Much comfort in that, I must say!

TREPLEV (*ironically*). Real talent! (*Wrathfully*) I have more talent than all of you put together if it comes to that! (*tears the bandage off his head*). You, with your hackneyed conventions, have usurped the supremacy in art and consider nothing real and legitimate but what you do yourselves; everything else you stifle and suppress. I don't believe in you! I don't believe in you or in him!

MADAME ARKADIN. Decadent!

TREPLEV. Get away to your charming theatre and act there in your paltry, stupid plays!

MADAME ARKADIN. I have never acted in such

plays. Let me alone! You are not capable of writing even a wretched burlesque! You are nothing but a Kiev shopman! living on other people!

TREPLEV. You miser!

MADAME ARKADIN. You ragged beggar!

(TREPLEV *sits down and weeps quietly.*)

MADAME ARKADIN. Nonentity! (*walking up and down in agitation*). Don't cry. . . . You mustn't cry (*weeps*). Don't . . . (*kisses him on the forehead, on the cheeks and on the head*). My dear child, forgive me. . . . Forgive your sinful mother. Forgive me, you know I am wretched.

TREPLEV (*puts his arms round her*). If only you knew! I have lost everything! She does not love me, and now I cannot write . . . all my hopes are gone. . . .

MADAME ARKADIN. Don't despair . . . Everything will come right. He is going away directly, she will love you again (*wipes away his tears*). Give over. We have made it up now.

TREPLEV (*kisses her hands*). Yes, mother.

MADAME ARKADIN (*tenderly*). Make it up with him too. You don't want a duel, do you?

TREPLEV. Very well. Only, mother, do allow me not to meet him. It's painful to me—it's more than I can bear. (*Enter* TRIGORIN.) Here he is . . . I am going . . . (*rapidly puts away the dressings in the cupboard*). The doctor will do the bandaging now.

TRIGORIN (*looking in a book*). Page 121 . . . lines 11 and 12. Here it is. (*Reads*) "If ever my life can be of use to you, come and take it."

(TREPLEV *picks up the bandage from the floor and goes out.*)

MADAME ARKADIN (*looking at her watch*). The horses will soon be here.

TRIGORIN (*to himself*). "If ever my life can be of use to you, come and take it."

MADAME ARKADIN. I hope all your things are packed?

TRIGORIN (*impatiently*). Yes, yes. (*Musing*) Why is it that I feel so much sorrow in that appeal from a pure soul and that it wrings my heart so painfully? "If ever my life can be of use to you, come and take it." (*To* MADAME ARKADIN) Let us stay one day longer.

(MADAME ARKADIN *shakes her head.*)

TRIGORIN. Let us stay!

MADAME ARKADIN. Darling, I know what keeps you here. But have control over yourself. You are a little intoxicated, try to be sober.

TRIGORIN. You be sober too, be sensible and reasonable, I implore you; look at it all as a true friend should. (*Presses her hand*) You are capable of sacrifice. Be a friend to me, let me be free!

MADAME ARKADIN (*in violent agitation*). Are you so enthralled?

TRIGORIN. I am drawn to her! Perhaps it is just what I need.

MADAME ARKADIN. The love of a provincial girl? Oh, how little you know yourself!

TRIGORIN. Sometimes people sleep as they walk—that's how it is with me, I am talking to you and yet I am asleep and dreaming of her. . . . I am possessed by sweet, marvellous dreams. . . . Let me be free. . . .

MADAME ARKADIN (*trembling*). No, no! I am

"The Maiden's Forest." It may be of use (*stretches*). So we are to go then? Again there will be railway carriages, stations, refreshment bars, mutton chops, conversations. . . .

SHAMRAEV (*enters*). I have the honour to announce, with regret, that the horses are ready. It's time, honoured lady, to set off for the station; the train comes in at five minutes past two. So please do me a favour, Irina Nikolaevna, do not forget to inquire what has become of the actor Suzdaltsev. Is he alive and well? We used to drink together at one time. . . . In "The Plundered Mail" he used to play incomparably . . . I remember the tragedian Izmaïlov, also a remarkable personality, acted with him in Elisavetograd. . . . Don't be in a hurry, honoured lady, you need not start for five minutes. Once they were acting conspirators in a melodrama and when they were suddenly discovered Izmaïlov had to say, "We are caught in a trap," but he said, "We are caught in a tap!" (*Laughs*) A tap!

(*While he is speaking* YAKOV *is busy looking after the luggage. The maid brings* MADAME ARKADIN *her hat, her coat, her umbrella and her gloves; they all help* MADAME ARKADIN *to put on her things. The man-cook looks in at the door on left and after some hesitation comes in. Enter* POLINA ANDREYEVNA, *then* SORIN *and* MEDVEDENKO.)

POLINA (*with a basket*). Here are some plums for the journey. . . . Very sweet ones. You may be glad to have something nice. . . .

MADAME ARKADIN. You are very kind, Polina Andreyevna.

POLINA. Good-bye, my dear! If anything has not been to your liking, forgive it (*weeps*).

MADAME ARKADIN (*embraces her*). Everything has been nice, everything! But you mustn't cry.

POLINA. The time flies so fast!

MADAME ARKADIN. There's no help for it.

SORIN (*in a great-coat with a cape to it, with his hat on and a stick in his hand, enters from door on left, crossing the stage*). Sister, it's time to start, or you may be too late after all. I am going to get into the carriage (*goes out*).

MEDVEDENKO. And I shall walk to the station . . . to see you off. I'll be there in no time . . . (*goes out*).

MADAME ARKADIN. Good-bye, dear friends. . . . If we are all alive and well, we shall meet again next summer. (*The maid, the cook and* YAKOV *kiss her hand.*) Don't forget me. (*Gives the cook a rouble*) Here's a rouble for the three of you.

THE COOK. We humbly thank you, madam! Good journey to you! We are very grateful for your kindness!

YAKOV. May God give you good luck!

SHAMRAEV. You might rejoice our hearts with a letter! Good-bye, Boris Alexeyevitch!

MADAME ARKADIN. Where is Konstantin? Tell him that I am starting; I must say good-bye. Well, don't remember evil against me. (*To* YAKOV) I gave the cook a rouble. It's for the three of you.

(*All go out on right. The stage is empty.*

Behind the scenes the noise that is usual when people are being seen off. The maid comes back to fetch the basket of plums from the table and goes out again.)

TRIGORIN (*coming back*). I have forgotten my stick. I believe it is out there, on the verandah (*goes and, at door on left, meets* NINA *who is coming in*). Is that you? We are going. . . .

NINA. I felt that we should see each other once more. (*Excitedly*) Boris Alexeyevitch, I have come to a decision, the die is cast, I am going on the stage. I shall be gone from here to-morrow; I am leaving my father, I am abandoning everything, I am beginning a new life. Like you, I am going . . . to Moscow. We shall meet there.

TRIGORIN (*looking round*). Stay at the "Slavyansky Bazaar" . . . Let me know at once . . . Molchanovka, Groholsky House. . . . I am in a hurry . . . (*a pause*).

NINA. One minute more. . . .

TRIGORIN (*in an undertone*). You are so lovely. . . . Oh, what happiness to think that we shall see each other soon! (*She sinks on his breast.*) I shall see again those wonderful eyes, that inexpressibly beautiful tender smile . . . those soft features, the expression of angelic purity. . . . My darling . . . (*a prolonged kiss*).

CURTAIN.

(*Between the Third and Fourth Acts there is an interval of two years.*)

ACT IV

One of the drawing-rooms in SORIN'S *house, which has been turned into a study for* KONSTANTIN TREPLEV. *On the right and left, doors leading to inner apartments. In the middle, glass door leading on to the verandah. Besides the usual drawing-room furniture there is, in corner on right, a writing-table, near door on left, a sofa, a bookcase and books in windows and on the chairs. Evening. There is a single lamp alight with a shade on it. It is half dark. There is the sound of the trees rustling, and the wind howling in the chimney. A watchman is tapping. Enter* MEDVEDENKO *and* MASHA.

MASHA (*calling*). Konstantin Gavrilitch! Konstantin Gavrilitch! (*Looking round*) No, there is no one here. The old man keeps asking every minute, where is Kostya, where is Kostya? He cannot live without him. . . .

MEDVEDENKO. He is afraid of being alone. (*Listening*) What awful weather! This is the second day of it.

MASHA (*turns up the lamp*). There are waves on the lake. Great big ones.

MEDVEDENKO. How dark it is in the garden! We ought to have told them to break up that stage in the garden. It stands as bare and ugly as a skeleton, and the curtain flaps in the wind. When I passed it yesterday evening, it seemed as though someone were crying in it.

MASHA. What next . . . (*a pause*).

MEDVEDENKO. Let us go home, Masha.

MASHA (*shakes her head*). I shall stay here for the night.

MEDVEDENKO (*in an imploring voice*). Masha, do come! Our baby must be hungry.

MASHA. Nonsense. Matryona will feed him (*a pause*).

MEDVEDENKO. I am sorry for him. He has been three nights now without his mother.

MASHA. You are a bore. In old days you used at least to discuss general subjects, but now it is only home, baby, home, baby—that's all one can get out of you.

MEDVEDENKO. Come along, Masha!

MASHA. Go by yourself.

MEDVEDENKO. Your father won't let me have a horse.

MASHA. Yes, he will. You ask, and he will.

MEDVEDENKO. Very well, I'll ask. Then you will come to-morrow?

MASHA (*taking a pinch of snuff*). Very well, to-morrow. How you pester me.

(*Enter* TREPLEV *and* POLINA ANDREYEVNA; TREPLEV *brings in pillows and a quilt, and* POLINA ANDREYEVNA *sheets and pillow-cases; they lay them on the sofa, then* TREPLEV *goes to his table and sits down.*)

MASHA. What's this for, mother?

POLINA. Pyotr Nikolayevitch asked us to make a bed for him in Kostya's room.

MASHA. Let me do it (*makes the bed*).

POLINA (*sighing*). Old people are like children (*goes up to the writing-table, and leaning on her elbow, looks at the manuscript; a pause*).

MEDVEDENKO. Well, I am going then. Good-bye, Masha (*kisses his wife's hand*). Good-bye, mother (*tries to kiss his mother-in-law's hand*).

POLINA (*with vexation*). Come, if you are going, go.

MEDVEDENKO. Good-bye, Konstantin Gavrilitch.

(TREPLEV *gives him his hand without speaking; MEDVEDENKO goes out.*)

POLINA (*looking at the MS.*). No one would have guessed or thought that you would have become a real author, Kostya. And now, thank God, they send you money from the magazines. (*Passes her hand over his hair*) And you have grown good-looking too. . . . Dear, good Kostya, do be a little kinder to my Mashenka!

MASHA (*as she makes the bed*). Leave him alone, mother.

POLINA (*to* TREPLEV). She is a nice little thing (*a pause*). A woman wants nothing, you know, Kostya, so long as you give her a kind look. I know from myself.

(TREPLEV *gets up from the table and walks away without speaking.*)

MASHA. Now you have made him angry. What induced you to pester him?

POLINA. I feel so sorry for you, Mashenka.

MASHA. Much use that is!

POLINA. My heart aches for you. I see it all, you know, I understand it all.

MASHA. It's all foolishness. There is no such thing as hopeless love except in novels. It's of no consequence. The only thing is one mustn't let oneself go and keep expecting something, waiting for the tide to turn. . . . When love gets into the heart there is nothing to be done but to clear it out. Here they promised to transfer my husband to another district. As soon as I am there, I shall forget it all . . . I shall tear it out of my heart.

(*Two rooms away a melancholy waltz is played.*)

POLINA. That's Kostya playing. He must be depressed.

MASHA (*noiselessly dances a few waltz steps*). The great thing, mother, is not to have him before one's eyes. If they only give my Semyon his transfer, trust me, I shall get over it in a month. It's all nonsense.

(*Door on left opens.* DORN *and* MEDVEDENKO *wheel in* SORIN *in his chair.*)

MEDVEDENKO. I have six of them at home now. And flour is two kopeks per pound.

DORN. You've got to look sharp to make both ends meet.

MEDVEDENKO. It's all very well for you to laugh. You've got more money than you know what to do with.

DORN. Money? After thirty years of practice, my boy, troublesome work during which I could not call my soul my own by day or by night, I only succeeded in saving two thousand roubles, and that I spent not long ago abroad. I have nothing.

MASHA (*to her husband*). You have not gone?

MEDVEDENKO (*guiltily*). Well, how can I when they won't let me have a horse?

MASHA (*with bitter vexation in an undertone*). I can't bear the sight of you.

(*The wheel-chair remains in the left half of the room;* POLINA ANDREYEVNA, MASHA *and* DORN *sit down beside it,* MEDVEDENKO *moves mournfully to one side.*)

DORN. What changes there have been here! The drawing-room has been turned into a study.

MASHA. It is more convenient for Konstantin Gavrilitch to work here. Whenever he likes, he can walk out into the garden and think there.

(*A watchman taps.*)

SORIN. Where is my sister?

DORN. She has gone to the station to meet Trigorin. She will be back directly.

SORIN. Since you thought it necessary to send for my sister, I must be dangerously ill. (*After a silence*) It's a queer thing, I am dangerously ill and here they don't give me any medicines.

DORN. Well, what would you like to have? Valerian drops? Soda? Quinine?

SORIN. Ah, he is at his moralising again! What an infliction it is! (*With a motion of his head towards the sofa*) Is that bed for me?

POLINA. Yes, it's for you, Pyotr Nikolayevitch.

SORIN. Thank you.

DORN (*hums*). "The moon is floating in the midnight sky."

SORIN. I want to give Kostya a subject for a story. It ought to be called "The Man who Wished"—*L'homme qui a voulu.* In my youth I wanted to become a literary man—and didn't; I wanted to speak well—and I spoke horribly badly, (*mimicking himself*) "and all the rest of it, and all that, and so on, and so forth" . . . and I would go plodding on and on, trying to sum up till I was in a regular perspiration; I wanted to get married—and I didn't; I always wanted to live in town and here I am ending my life in the country—and so on.

DORN. I wanted to become an actual civil councillor—and I have.

SORIN (*laughs*). That I had no hankerings after. That happened of itself.

DORN. To be expressing dissatisfaction with life at sixty-two is really ungracious, you know.

SORIN. What a persistent fellow he is! You might understand that one wants to live!

DORN. That's just frivolity. It's the law of nature that every life must have an end.

SORIN. You argue like a man who has had enough. You are satisfied and so you are indifferent to life, nothing matters to you. But even you will be afraid to die.

DORN. The dread of death is an animal fear. One must overcome it. A rational fear of death is only possible for those who believe in eternal life and are conscious of their sins. And you, in the first place, don't believe, and, in the second, what sins have you to worry about? You have served in the courts of justice for twenty-five years—that's all.

SORIN (*laughs*). Twenty-eight. . . .

(TREPLEV *comes in and sits down on a stool at* SORIN'S *feet.* MASHA *never takes her eyes off him.*)

DORN. We are hindering Konstantin Gavrilitch from working.

TREPLEV. Oh no, it doesn't matter (*a pause*).

MEDVEDENKO. Allow me to ask you, doctor, what town did you like best abroad?

DORN. Genoa.

TREPLEV. Why Genoa?

DORN. The life in the streets is so wonderful there. When you go out of the hotel in the evening, the whole street is packed with people. You wander aimlessly zigzagging about among the crowd, backwards and forwards; you live with it, are psychologically at one with it and begin almost to believe that a world-soul is really possible, such as was acted by Nina Zaretchny in your play. And, by the way, where is she now? How is she getting on?

TREPLEV. I expect she is quite well.

DORN. I was told that she was leading a rather peculiar life. How was that?

TREPLEV. That's a long story, doctor.

DORN. Well, tell it us shortly (*a pause*).

TREPLEV. She ran away from home and had an affair with Trigorin. You know that?

DORN. I know.

TREPLEV. She had a child. The child died.

Trigorin got tired of her and went back to his old ties, as might have been expected. Though, indeed, he had never abandoned them, but in his weak-willed way contrived to keep both going. As far as I can make out from what I have heard, Nina's private life was a complete failure.

DORN. And the stage?

TREPLEV. I fancy that was worse still. She made her début at some holiday place near Moscow, then went to the provinces. All that time I did not lose sight of her, and wherever she went I followed her. She always took big parts, but she acted crudely, without taste, screamingly, with violent gestures. There were moments when she uttered a cry successfully or died successfully, but they were only moments.

DORN. Then she really has some talent?

TREPLEV. It was difficult to make it out. I suppose she has. I saw her but she would not see me, and the servants would not admit me at the hotel. I understood her state of mind and did not insist on seeing her (*a pause*). What more can I tell you? Afterwards, when I was back at home, I had some letters from her—warm, intelligent, interesting letters. She did not complain, but I felt that she was profoundly unhappy; every line betrayed sick overstrained nerves. And her imagination is a little unhinged. She signed herself the Sea-gull. In Pushkin's "Mermaid" the miller says that he is a raven, and in the same way in her letters she kept repeating that she was a sea-gull. Now she is here.

DORN. Here? How do you mean?

TREPLEV. In the town, staying at an inn. She has been there for five days. I did go to see her, and Marya Ilyinishna here went too, but she won't see anyone. Semyon Semyonitch declares he saw her yesterday afternoon in the fields a mile and a half from here.

MEDVEDENKO. Yes, I saw her. She went in that direction, towards the town. I bowed to her and asked her why she did not come to see us. She said she would come.

TREPLEV. She won't come (*a pause*). Her father and stepmother refuse to recognise her. They have put watchmen about so that she may not even go near the house (*walks away with the doctor towards the writing table*). How easy it is to be a philosopher on paper, doctor, and how difficult it is in life!

SORIN. She was a charming girl.

DORN. What?

SORIN. She was a charming girl, I say. Actual Civil Councillor Sorin was positively in love with her for a time.

DORN. The old Lovelace.

(SHAMRAEV'S *laugh is heard.*)

POLINA. I fancy our people have come back from the station. . . .

TREPLEV. Yes, I hear mother.

(*Enter* MADAME ARKADIN, TRIGORIN *and with them* SHAMRAEV.)

SHAMRAEV (*as he enters*). We all grow old and dilapidated under the influence of the elements, while you, honoured lady, are still young . . . a light blouse, sprightliness, grace. . . .

MADAME ARKADIN. You want to bring me ill-luck again, you tiresome man!

TRIGORIN. How do you do, Pyotr Nikolayevitch! So you are still poorly? That's bad! (*Seeing* MASHA, *joyfully*) Marya Ilyinishna!

MASHA. You know me, do you? (*shakes hands*).

TRIGORIN. Married?

MASHA. Long ago.

TRIGORIN. Are you happy? (*Bows to* DORN *and* MEDVEDENKO, *then hesitatingly approaches* TREPLEV) Irina Nikolayevna has told me that you have forgotten the past and are no longer angry.

(TREPLEV *holds out his hand.*)

MADAME ARKADIN (*to her son*). Boris Alexeyevitch has brought the magazine with your new story in it.

TREPLEV (*taking the magazine, to* TRIGORIN). Thank you, you are very kind. (*They sit down.*)

TRIGORIN. Your admirers send their greetings to you. . . . In Petersburg and Moscow there is great interest in your work and I am continually being asked questions about you. People ask what you are like, how old you are, whether you are dark or fair. Everyone imagines, for some reason, that you are no longer young. And no one knows your real name, as you always publish under a pseudonym. You are as mysterious as the Iron Mask.

TREPLEV. Will you be able to make a long stay?

TRIGORIN. No, I think I must go back to Moscow to-morrow. I am obliged to. I am in a hurry to finish my novel, and besides, I have promised something for a collection of tales that is being published. It's the old story, in fact.

(*While they are talking* MADAME ARKADIN *and* POLINA ANDREYEVNA *put a card-table in the middle of the room and open it out.* SHAMRAEV *lights candles and sets chairs. A game of loto is brought out of the cupboard.*)

TRIGORIN. The weather has not given me a friendly welcome. There is a cruel wind. If it has dropped by to-morrow morning I shall go to the lake to fish. And I must have a look at the garden and that place where—you remember?—your play was acted. I've got a subject for a story, I only want to revive my recollections of the scene in which it is laid.

MASHA (*to her father*). Father, let my husband have a horse! He must get home.

SHAMRAEV (*mimicking*). Must get home—a horse! (*Sternly*) You can see for yourself: they have just been to the station. I can't send them out again.

MASHA. But there are other horses. (*Seeing that her father says nothing, waves her hand*) There's no doing anything with you.

MEDVEDENKO. I can walk, Masha. Really. . . .

POLINA (*with a sigh*). Walk in such weather . . . (*sits down to the card-table*). Come, friends.

MEDVEDENKO. It is only four miles. Good-bye (*kisses his wife's hand*). Good-bye, mother. (*His mother-in-law reluctantly holds out her hand for him to kiss.*) I wouldn't trouble anyone, but the baby . . . (*bows to the company*). Good-bye . . . (*goes out with a guilty step*).

SHAMRAEV. He can walk right enough. He's not a general.

POLINA (*tapping on the table*). Come, friends. Don't let us waste time, we shall soon be called to supper.

(SHAMRAEV, MASHA *and* DORN *sit down at the table.*)

MADAME ARKADIN (*to* TRIGORIN). When the long autumn evenings come on, they play loto here. Look, it's the same old loto that we had when our mother used to play with us, when we were children. Won't you have a game before supper? (*sits down to the table with* TRIGORIN). It's a dull game, but it is not so bad when you are used to it (*deals three cards to everyone*).

TREPLEV (*turning the pages of the magazine*). He has read his own story, but he has not even cut mine (*puts the magazine down on the writing-table, then goes towards door on left; as he passes his mother he kisses her on the head*).

MADAME ARKADIN. And you, Kostya?

TREPLEV. Excuse me, I would rather not . . . I am going out (*goes out*).

MADAME ARKADIN. The stake is ten kopeks. Put it down for me, doctor, will you?

DORN. Right.

MASHA. Has everyone put down their stakes? I begin . . . Twenty-two.

MADAME ARKADIN. Yes.

MASHA. Three!

DORN. Right!

MASHA. Did you play three? Eight! Eighty-one! Ten!

SHAMRAEV. Don't be in a hurry!

MADAME ARKADIN. What a reception I had in Harkov! My goodness! I feel dizzy with it still.

MASHA. Thirty-four!

(*A melancholy waltz is played behind the scenes.*)

MADAME ARKADIN. The students gave me an ovation. . . . Three baskets of flowers . . . two wreaths and this, see (*unfastens a brooch on her throat and lays it on the table*).

SHAMRAEV. Yes, that is a thing. . . .

MASHA. Fifty!

DORN. Exactly fifty?

MADAME ARKADIN. I had a wonderful dress. . . . Whatever I don't know, I do know how to dress.

POLINA. Kostya is playing the piano; he is depressed, poor fellow.

SHAMRAEV. He is awfully abused in the newspapers.

MASHA. Seventy-seven!

MADAME ARKADIN. As though that mattered!

TRIGORIN. He never quite comes off. He has not yet hit upon his own medium. There is always something queer and vague, at times almost like delirium. Not a single living character.

MASHA. Eleven!

MADAME ARKADIN (*looking round at* SORIN). Petrusha, are you bored? (*a pause*). He is asleep.

DORN. The actual civil councillor is asleep.

MASHA. Seven! Ninety!

TRIGORIN. If I lived in such a place, beside a

lake, do you suppose I should write? I should overcome this passion and should do nothing but fish.

MASHA. Twenty-eight!

TRIGORIN. Catching perch is so delightful!

DORN. Well, I believe in Konstantin Gavrilitch. There is something in him! There is something in him! He thinks in images; his stories are vivid, full of colour and they affect me strongly. The only pity is that he has not got definite aims. He produces an impression and that's all, but you can't get far with nothing but an impression. Irina Nikolayevna, are you glad that your son is a writer?

MADAME ARKADIN. Only fancy, I have not read anything of his yet. I never have time.

MASHA. Twenty-six!

(TREPLEV *comes in quietly and sits down at his table.*)

SHAMRAEV (*to* TRIGORIN). We have still got something here belonging to you, Boris Alexeyevitch.

TRIGORIN. What's that?

SHAMRAEV. Konstantin Gavrilitch shot a seagull and you asked me to get it stuffed for you.

TRIGORIN. I don't remember! (*Pondering*) I don't remember!

MASHA. Sixty-six! One!

TREPLEV (*flinging open the window, listens*). How dark it is! I don't know why I feel so uneasy.

MADAME ARKADIN. Kostya, shut the window, there's a draught.

(TREPLEV *shuts the window.*)

MASHA. Eighty-eight!

TRIGORIN. The game is mine!

MADAME ARKADIN (*gaily*). Bravo, bravo!

SHAMRAEV. Bravo!

MADAME ARKADIN. That man always has luck in everything (*gets up*). And now let us go and have something to eat. Our great man has not dined to-day. We will go on again after supper. (*To her son*) Kostya, leave your manuscripts and come to supper.

TREPLEV. I don't want any, mother, I am not hungry.

MADAME ARKADIN. As you like. (*Wakes* SORIN) Petrusha, supper! (*Takes* SHAMRAEV'S *arm*) I'll tell you about my reception in Harkov.

(POLINA ANDREYEVNA *puts out the candles on the table. Then she and* DORN *wheel the chair. All go out by door on left; only* TREPLEV, *sitting at the writing-table, is left on the stage.*)

TREPLEV (*settling himself to write; runs through what he has written already*). I have talked so much about new forms and now I feel that little by little I am falling into a convention myself. (*Reads*) "The placard on the wall proclaimed. . . . The pale face in its setting of dark hair." Proclaimed, setting. That's stupid (*scratches out*). I will begin where the hero is awakened by the patter of the rain, and throw out all the rest. The description of the moonlight evening is long and over elaborate. Trigorin has worked out methods for himself, it's easy for him now. . . . With him the broken bottle neck glitters on the dam and the mill-wheel casts a black shadow—and there you have the moonlight night, while I have the tremulous light, and the soft twinkling of the stars, and the far-away strains of the piano dying away in the still fragrant air. . . . It's agonising (*a pause*). I come more and more to the conviction that it is not a question of new and old forms, but that what matters is that a man should write without thinking about forms at all, write because it springs freely from his soul. (*There is a tap at the window nearest to the table*) What is that? (*looks out of window*). There is nothing to be seen . . . (*opens the glass door and looks out into the garden*). Someone ran down the steps. (*Calls*) Who is there? (*Goes out and can be heard walking rapidly along the verandah; returns half a minute later with* NINA ZARETCHNY). Nina, Nina!

(NINA *lays her head on his breast and weeps with subdued sobs.*)

TREPLEV (*moved*). Nina! Nina! It's you . . . you. . . . It's as though I had foreseen it, all day long my heart has been aching and restless (*takes off her hat and cape*). Oh, my sweet, my precious, she has come at last! Don't let us cry, don't let us!

NINA. There is someone here.

TREPLEV. No one.

NINA. Lock the doors, someone may come in.

TREPLEV. No one will come in.

NINA. I know Irina Nikolayevna is here. Lock the doors.

TREPLEV (*locks the door on right, goes to door*

on left). There is no lock on this one, I'll put a chair against it (*puts an armchair against the door*). Don't be afraid, no one will come.

NINA (*looking intently into his face*). Let me look at you. (*Looking round*) It's warm, it's nice. . . . In old days this was the drawing-room. Am I very much changed?

TREPLEV. Yes. . . . You are thinner and your eyes are bigger. Nina, how strange it is that I should be seeing you. Why would not you let me see you? Why haven't you come all this time? I know you have been here almost a week. . . . I have been to you several times every day; I stood under your window like a beggar.

NINA. I was afraid that you might hate me. I dream every night that you look at me and don't know me. If only you knew! Ever since I came I have been walking here . . . by the lake. I have been near your house many times and could not bring myself to enter it. Let us sit down. (*They sit down.*) Let us sit down and talk and talk. It's nice here, it's warm and snug. Do you hear the wind? There's a passage in Turgenev, "Well for the man on such a night who sits under the shelter of home, who has a warm corner in safety." I am a sea-gull. . . . No, that's not it (*rubs her forehead*). What was I saying? Yes . . . Turgenev . . . "And the Lord help all homeless wanderers!" . . . It doesn't matter (*sobs*).

TREPLEV. Nina, you are crying again. . . . Nina!

NINA. Never mind, it does me good . . . I haven't cried for two years. Yesterday, late in the evening, I came into the garden to see whether our stage was still there. It is still standing. I cried for the first time after two years and it eased the weight on my heart and made it lighter. You see, I am not crying now (*takes him by the hand*). And so now you are an author. . . . You are an author, I am an actress. . . . We too have been drawn into the whirlpool. I lived joyously, like a child—I woke up singing in the morning; I loved you and dreamed of fame, and now? Early to-morrow morning I must go to Yelets third-class . . . with peasants, and at Yelets the cultured tradesmen will pester me with attentions. Life is a coarse business!

TREPLEV. Why to Yelets?

NINA. I have taken an engagement for the whole winter. It is time to go.

TREPLEV. Nina, I cursed you, I hated you, I tore up your letters and photographs, but I was conscious every minute that my soul is bound to yours for ever. It's not in my power to leave off loving you, Nina. Ever since I lost you and began to get my work published my life has been unbearable—I am wretched. . . . My youth was, as it were, torn away all at once and it seems to me as though I have lived for ninety years already. I call upon you, I kiss the earth on which you have walked; wherever I look I see your face, that tender smile that lighted up the best days of my life. . . .

NINA (*distractedly*). Why does he talk like this, why does he talk like this?

TREPLEV. I am alone in the world, warmed by no affection. I am as cold as though I were in a cellar, and everything I write is dry, hard and gloomy. Stay here, Nina, I entreat you, or let me go with you !

(NINA *rapidly puts on her hat and cape.*)

TREPLEV. Nina, why is this ? For God's sake, Nina ! (*looks at her as she puts her things on ; a pause*).

NINA. My horses are waiting at the gate. Don't see me off, I'll go alone. . . . (*Through her tears*) Give me some water. . . .

TREPLEV (*gives her some water*). Where are you going now ?

NINA. To the town (*a pause*). Is Irina Nikolayevna here ?

TREPLEV. Yes. . . . Uncle was taken worse on Thursday and we telegraphed for her.

NINA. Why do you say that you kissed the earth on which I walked ? I ought to be killed. (*Bends over the table*) I am so tired ! If I could rest . . . if I could rest ! (*Raising her head*) I am a sea-gull. . . . No, that's not it. I am an actress. Oh, well ! (*Hearing* MADAME ARKADIN *and* TRIGORIN *laughing, she listens, then runs to door on left and looks through the keyhole*). He is here too. . . . (*Turning back to* TREPLEV) Oh, well . . . it doesn't matter . . . no. . . . He did not believe in the stage, he always laughed at my dreams and little by little I left off believing in it too, and lost heart. . . . And then I was fretted by love and jealousy, and continually anxious over my little one. . . . I grew petty and trivial, I acted stupidly. . . . I did not know what to do with my arms, I did not know how to stand on the stage, could not control my voice. You can't understand what it feels like when one knows one is acting disgracefully. I am a sea-gull. No, that's not it. . . . Do you remember you shot a sea-gull? A man came by chance, saw it and, just to pass the time, destroyed it. . . . A subject for a short story. . . . That's not it, though (*rubs her forehead*). What was I saying? . . . I am talking of the stage. Now I am not like that. I am a real actress, I act with enjoyment, with enthusiasm, I am intoxicated when I am on the stage and feel that I am splendid. And since I have been here, I keep walking about and thinking, thinking and feeling that my soul is getting stronger every day. Now I know, I understand, Kostya, that in our work—in acting or writing—what matters is not fame, not glory, not what I dreamed of, but knowing how to be patient. To bear one's cross and have faith. I have faith and it all doesn't hurt so much, and when I think of my vocation I am not afraid of life.

TREPLEV (*mournfully*). You have found your path, you know which way you are going, but I am still floating in a chaos of dreams and images, not knowing what use it is to anyone. I have no faith and don't know what my vocation is.

NINA (*listening*). 'Sh-sh . . . I am going. Good-bye. When I become a great actress, come and look at me. Will you promise? But now . . . (*presses his hand*) it's late. I can hardly stand on my feet. . . . I am worn out and hungry. . . .

TREPLEV. Stay, I'll give you some supper.

NINA. No, no. . . . Don't see me off, I will go by

myself. My horses are close by. . . . So she brought him with her? Well, it doesn't matter. When you see Trigorin, don't say anything to him. . . . I love him! I love him even more than before. . . . A subject for a short story . . . I love him, I love him passionately, I love him to despair. It was nice in old days, Kostya! Do you remember? How clear, warm, joyous and pure life was, what feelings we had—feelings like tender, exquisite flowers. . . . Do you remember? (*Recites*) "Men, lions, eagles, and partridges, horned deer, geese, spiders, silent fish that dwell in the water, star-fishes, and creatures which cannot be seen by the eye—all living things, all living things, all living things, have completed their cycle of sorrow, are extinct. . . . For thousands of years the earth has borne no living creature on its surface, and this poor moon lights its lamp in vain. On the meadow the cranes no longer waken with a cry and there is no sound of the May beetles in the lime trees . . ." (*impulsively embraces* TREPLEV *and runs out of the glass door*).

TREPLEV (*after a pause*). It will be a pity if someone meets her in the garden and tells mother. It may upset mother. . . .

(*He spends two minutes in tearing up all his manuscripts and throwing them under the table; then unlocks the door on right and goes out.*)

DORN (*trying to open the door on left*). Strange. The door seems to be locked . . . (*comes in and puts the armchair in its place*). An obstacle race.

(*Enter* MADAME ARKADIN *and* POLINA ANDREYEVNA, *behind them* YAKOV *carrying a tray with bottles;* MASHA; *then* SHAMRAEV *and* TRIGORIN.)

MADAME ARKADIN. Put the claret and the beer for Boris Alexeyevitch here on the table. We will play as we drink it. Let us sit down, friends.

POLINA (*to* YAKOV). Bring tea too at the same time (*lights the candles and sits down to the card table*).

SHAMRAEV (*leads* TRIGORIN *to the cupboard*). Here's the thing I was speaking about just now (*takes the stuffed sea-gull from the cupboard*). This is what you ordered.

TRIGORIN (*looking at the sea-gull*). I don't remember it. (*Musing*) I don't remember.

(*The sound of a shot coming from right of stage; everyone starts.*)

MADAME ARKADIN (*frightened*). What's that?

DORN. That's nothing. It must be something in my medicine-chest that has gone off. Don't be anxious (*goes out at door on right, comes back in half a minute*). That's what it is. A bottle of ether has exploded. (*Hums*) "I stand before thee enchanted again. . . ."

MADAME ARKADIN (*sitting down to the table*). Ough, how frightened I was. It reminded me of how . . . (*hides her face in her hands*). It made me quite dizzy. . . .

DORN (*turning over the leaves of the magazine, to* TRIGORIN). There was an article in this two months ago—a letter from America—and I wanted to ask you, among other things (*puts his arm round

TRIGORIN'S *waist and leads him to the footlights*) as I am very much interested in the question. . . . (*In a lower tone, dropping his voice*) Get Irina Nikolayevna away somehow. The fact is, Konstantin Gavrilitch has shot himself. . . .

CURTAIN.

THE BEAR

A JEST IN ONE ACT

First performed in 1889.

CHARACTERS IN THE PLAY.

YELENA IVANOVNA POPOV (*a widow with dimples in her cheeks, owner of an estate in the country*).
GRIGORY STEPANITCH SMIRNOV (*a middle-aged Landowner*).
LUKA (MADAME POPOV'S *old manservant*).

The action takes place in a drawing-room in MADAME POPOV'S *house.*

THE BEAR

A JEST IN ONE ACT

MADAME POPOV (*in deep mourning, keeps her eyes fixed on a photograph*) *and* LUKA.

LUKA. It's not right, madam. . . . You are simply killing yourself. . . . The cook and the housemaid have gone to the wood to pick strawberries, every breathing thing rejoices, the very cat, even she knows how to enjoy herself and walks about the yard catching birds, while you sit all day indoors as though you were in a nunnery and have no pleasure in anything. Yes, indeed! If you come to think of it, it's nearly a year since you've been out of the house!

MADAME POPOV. And I shall never go out. . . . Why should I? My life is over. He lies in his grave; I have buried myself within four walls. . . . We are both dead.

LUKA. Well, there it is! I don't like to hear it. Nikolay Mihailitch is dead, so it had to be, it is God's will. The kingdom of heaven be his! . . . You have grieved, and that's enough; you must know when to stop. You can't weep and wear mourning all your life. I buried my old woman, too, in my time. . . . Well, I was grieved and cried for a month or so, and that was enough for her; but if I had been doleful all my life, it is more than the old woman herself was worth. (*Sighs*) You have forgotten all your neighbours. . . . You don't go out yourself or receive visitors. We live like spiders, if I may say so—we don't see the light of day. The mice have eaten my livery. . . . It's not as though you had no nice people about you: the district is full of gentry. . . . There's a regiment at Ryblovo—the officers are perfect sugar-plums, a sight for sore eyes! And in the camp there is a ball every Friday, and the band plays almost every day. . . . Ah! madam, my dear, you are young and lovely, blooming like a rose—you have only to live and enjoy yourself. . . . Beauty won't last all your life, you know. In another ten years you may want to be as gay as a peacock and dazzle the officers, but then it will be too late. . . .

MADAME POPOV (*resolutely*). I beg you never to speak like that to me! You know that ever since Nikolay Mihailitch died life has lost all value for me. It appears to you that I am alive, but it is only an appearance! I have taken a vow not to put off this mourning, nor to look upon the world outside as long as I live. . . . Do you hear? May his shade see how I love him! . . . Yes, I know it was no secret to you: he was often unjust to me, cruel and . . . and even unfaithful; but I will be true to the grave, and will show him how I can love. Yonder, on the other side of the grave, he will see me just the same as I was before his death. . . .

LUKA. Instead of talking like that you had better go for a walk in the garden, or order Toby or Giant to be put into the carriage and go to visit your neighbours. . . .

MADAME POPOV. Ach! (*weeps*).

LUKA. Madam! My dear! What is it? Christ be with you!

MADAME POPOV. He was so fond of Toby! He always used to drive him when he went to the Kortchagins or the Vlassovs. How wonderfully he drove! What grace there was in his figure when he tugged at the reins with all his might! Do you remember? Toby, Toby! Tell them to give him an extra gallon of oats to-day!

LUKA. Yes, madam.

(*An abrupt ring at the bell.*)

MADAME POPOV (*starts*). Who is that? Say that I see no one.

LUKA. Yes, madam (*goes out*).

MADAME POPOV (*looking at the photograph*). You will see, Nicolas, how I can love and forgive . . . . My love will die only with me when my poor heart leaves off beating (*laughing through her tears*). And aren't you ashamed? I am a good girl—a true wife. I have locked myself up, and will be true to you to the grave, while you . . . . aren't you ashamed, you chubby? You deceived me, you made scenes, left me alone for weeks together. . . .

(LUKA *enters in a fluster.*)

LUKA. Madam, there is someone asking for you. He wants to see you.

MADAME POPOV. But didn't you tell him that since my husband's death I see no one?

LUKA. I did, but he won't listen; he says it is on very urgent business.

MADAME POPOV. I see no-bo-dy!

LUKA. I told him so, but . . . he is a regular devil. He swears and just shoves himself into the room . . . he is in the dining-room now.

MADAME POPOV (*irritably*). Oh, very well! Show him in. How rude!

(LUKA *goes out.*)

MADAME POPOV. How wearisome these people are! What do they want of me? Why should they disturb my peace? (*sighs*). It seems I shall really have to go into a nunnery . . . (*Ponders*) Yes, a nunnery. . . .

(*Enter* LUKA *with* SMIRNOV.)

SMIRNOV (*as he enters, to* LUKA). Blockhead, you are too fond of talking! Ass! (*Seeing* MADAME POPOV, *with dignity*) Madam, I have the honour to introduce myself: Gregory Stepanitch Smirnov, landowner and retired lieutenant of artillery. I am compelled to trouble you about a very important matter.

MADAME POPOV (*not offering her hand*). What can I do for you?

SMIRNOV. Your late husband, whom I had the honour of knowing, owed me twelve hundred roubles on two bills. As I have to-morrow to pay my interest to the land bank, I am obliged to ask you to repay me that sum to-day.

MADAME POPOV. Twelve hundred! . . . And what did my husband owe you that money for?

SMIRNOV. He bought oats from me.

MADAME POPOV (*sighing, to* LUKA). Don't forget, Luka, to tell them to give Toby an extra gallon of oats (LUKA *goes out. To* SMIRNOV) If

Nikolay Mihailitch owed you money, of course I will pay it, but you must please excuse me—I haven't the cash in hand to-day. My steward will be coming back from the town the day after to-morrow, and I will tell him to pay you what is owing; but till then I cannot do what you want. . . . Besides, it is exactly seven months to-day since my husband died, and I am in such a state of mind that I don't feel equal to attending to money matters.

SMIRNOV. And I am in such a state of mind that if I don't pay my interest to-morrow I shall have to put a bullet through my brains. They'll sell up my estate.

MADAME POPOV. The day after to-morrow you shall have the money.

SMIRNOV. I want the money, not the day after to-morrow, but to-day.

MADAME POPOV. Excuse me, I cannot pay you to-day.

SMIRNOV. And I can't wait till the day after to-morrow.

MADAME POPOV. What am I to do if I haven't the money?

SMIRNOV. Then you can't pay it?

MADAME POPOV. I cannot.

SMIRNOV. H'm! Is that your final answer?

MADAME POPOV. Yes.

SMIRNOV. The final? Positively?

MADAME POPOV. Positively.

SMIRNOV. Very much obliged to you. I'll make a note of it (*shrugs his shoulders*). And I am expected to keep cool! I met the excise officer on the road just now, and he asked me, "Why are you always so angry, Grigory Stepanitch?" Upon my soul, how can I help being angry? I am in deadly need of money. I set off almost before daylight yesterday morning, I went round to all who owed me money, and not one has paid me! I am as tired as a dog. Goodness knows where I spent the night—in a wretched Jewish pot-house, beside a barrel of vodka. . . . At last I get here, over fifty miles from home, hoping to be paid my money, and all I am offered is a state of mind! How am I to keep my temper?

MADAME POPOV. I believe I have told you distinctly that when my steward comes back from the town you will be paid.

SMIRNOV. I have come to see you, and not your steward! What the devil—excuse the expression—do I want with your steward?

MADAME POPOV. Excuse me, sir, I am not accustomed to such strange expressions and such a tone. I will not listen to you (*goes out quickly*).

SMIRNOV. Upon my soul! A state of mind! . . . It's seven months since her husband died. . . . But am I to pay the interest, or not? I ask you, am I to pay the interest, or not? To be sure, your husband is dead, and you are in a state of mind, and all sorts of nonsense. Your steward has gone off somewhere—the devil take him!—but what am I to do? Fly away from my creditors on a balloon, or what? Or run and smash my skull against the wall? I went to Gruzdyov—not at home. Yaroshevitch was in hiding. With Kuritsin I had an awful row, and nearly flung him out of window. Mazutov had a bilious attack, and this one has got a state of mind! Not one of the wretches has paid me! And all because I have been too soft with them—because I am a noodle, a rag, an old woman! I've been too gentle with them. But wait a bit! I'll show you what I can do. I won't let them make a fool of me, damnation take it! I'll stay and stick on here till she does pay. Brr! How cross I feel to-day! I am in such a rage that I'm twitching all over, and I can hardly breathe. . . . Phew! Hang it, I feel positively sick! (*Shouts*) Hi, there!

(*Enter* LUKA.)

LUKA. What is it?

SMIRNOV. Give me some kvass or some water.

(LUKA *goes out.*)

SMIRNOV. Yes, what logic! A man is in deadly need of money—nothing left but to hang himself—and she won't pay because, if you please, she is not equal to attending to money matters! . . . Typical petticoat logic! That is why I never like, and never have liked, talking to women. I'd rather sit on a barrel of gunpowder than talk to a woman! Brr! I am chicken-flesh all over—that feminine creature has put me in such a rage! I have only to see a poetic being like that in the distance for my legs to begin twitching with fury. I feel like shouting "Help!"

(LUKA *enters and gives him water.*)

LUKA. My lady is unwell and sees no one.

SMIRNOV. Be off!

(LUKA *goes out.*)

SMIRNOV. Unwell and sees no one! Very good,

you needn't. . . . I'll stay on and sit here till you do pay me. If you are ill a week, I'll stay here for a week. If you are ill for a year, I'll stay for a year. . . . I'll get my own back, my good woman! You won't touch me with your mourning and the dimples in your cheeks. We all know about those dimples! (*Shouts out of window*) Semyon! Take the horses out. We shan't be leaving just directly. I am staying here. Tell them at the stable to give the horses a feed of oats. You've let the left trace horse get its legs into the reins again, you brute! (*Mimicking*) It's a—a—all right. I'll show you if it's all right! (*moves away from the window*). It's a bad look-out. The heat is insufferable, no one will pay, I had a bad night, and now this mourning female with her state of mind! . . . My head aches. . . . Shall I have some vodka? Perhaps I will. (*Shouts*) Hi, there!

(*Enter* LUKA.)

LUKA. What is it?

SMIRNOV. Bring me a glass of vodka. (LUKA *goes out*). Ough! (*sits down and examines himself*). I must say, I am a nice sight! Covered with dust, muddy boots, unwashed, uncombed, straws on my waistcoat! The lady thought I was a highwayman, I expect (*yawns*). . . . It's not quite polite to come into a drawing-room looking like this—but there, it doesn't matter. I am not a visitor—I am a creditor and there is no regulation dress for a creditor.

(*Enter* LUKA.)

LUKA (*giving him vodka*). You take liberties, sir.

SMIRNOV (*angrily*). What?

LUKA. Nothing. I only . . .

SMIRNOV. To whom are you speaking? Shut up!

LUKA (*aside*). Well, here's an infliction! It's an ill wind brought him (*goes out*).

SMIRNOV. Ach, how furious I am! I feel as though I should like to pound the whole world into powder. . . . I feel positively sick. . . . (*Shouts*) Hi, there!

(MADAME POPOV *enters, looking down.*)

MADAME POPOV. Sir, in my solitude I have long been unused to the human voice, and cannot endure shouting. I beg you most earnestly not to disturb my peace.

SMIRNOV. Pay me my money, and I will go.

MADAME POPOV. I've told you in plain Russian I have no money in hand at the moment. Wait till the day after to-morrow.

SMIRNOV. I too had the honour of telling you in plain Russian that I need the money, not the day after to-morrow, but to-day. If you don't pay me to-day, I shall have to hang myself to-morrow.

MADAME POPOV. But what am I to do if I have no money? How strange it is!

SMIRNOV. So you won't pay me at once . . . you won't?

MADAME POPOV. I can't. . . .

SMIRNOV. In that case I shall stop here, and shall go on staying here till I get it (*sits down*). You will pay me the day after to-morrow! Very good! I shall sit here till the day after to-morrow.

I shall sit here like this . . . (*leaps up*). I ask you, am I obliged to pay my interest to-morrow, or not? Or do you think I am joking?

MADAME POPOV. Sir, I beg you not to shout! This is not a stable.

SMIRNOV. I am not asking you about a stable.. I am asking—have I got to pay my interest to-morrow, or not?

MADAME POPOV. You don't know how to behave in the society of ladies.

SMIRNOV. Yes, I do know how to behave in the society of ladies.

MADAME POPOV. No, you don't! You are a coarse, ill-bred man. Decent people don't speak like that to ladies.

SMIRNOV. Oh, that's curious! How would you like me to speak to you? In French, or what? (*Growing angry and speaking with a lisp*) *Madame, je vous prie,* how happy I am that you are not paying me my money. Ach, *pardon* for having troubled you! What a lovely day it is? And how that mourning suits you! (*bows and scrapes*).

MADAME POPOV. That's rude and not clever.

SMIRNOV (*mimicking her*). Rude and not clever! I don't know how to behave in the society of ladies! Madam, I have seen more women in my day than you have sparrows. I have fought three duels over women. I have thrown over twelve women, and nine have thrown me over. Yes! There was a time when I played the fool—when I was all sentiment and honey, did the polite, was all bowing and scraping. . . . I loved and suffered, sighed at the moon, was all thrills and raptures.

. . . I loved passionately, frantically in all sorts of ways, confound me!—chattered like a magpie about the rights of women, spent half my fortune on the tender passion; but now—no, thank you! You won't get round me now. I've had enough. Black eyes, eyes full of passion, crimson lips, dimples, moonlight, whisperings, timid breathing —I would not give a brass farthing for all that, madam! Present company excepted, of course, all women, young and old, are affected, mincing, gossiping, spiteful, liars to the marrow of their bones, trivial, petty, pitiless; their logic is most revolting, and as for this department (*slaps himself on the forehead*)—excuse me for my candour—a sparrow can give points to any philosopher in petticoats! One looks at some poetical creature, all in muslin, an ethereal being, a goddess, a million raptures, but if one peeps into her soul she is the most commonplace crocodile! (*takes hold of the back of a chair; the chair cracks and breaks*). But what's most revolting is that this crocodile, for some reason, imagines that her *chef-d'œuvre*, her monopoly and privilege, is the tender passion! But, damnation take me, you may hang me on this nail, head downwards, if a woman has ever been capable of loving anyone but a lap-dog! In love all she can do is to whine and whimper. While a man suffers and makes sacrifices, all her love expresses itself in trailing her skirts and trying to keep a tight hold on him. You have the misfortune to be a woman, and so you know a woman's nature from yourself. Tell me honestly, have you ever in your life seen a woman who was sincere, true, and constant? You haven't! None but old women and frights are true and constant. It is easier to find a cat with horns or a white snipe than a constant woman!

MADAME POPOV. Allow me to ask, then, who is true and constant in love according to you? Not man, surely!

SMIRNOV. Yes, man.

MADAME POPOV. Man! (*laughs maliciously*). Man true and constant in love! That's something new, I must say. (*Hotly*) What right have you to say such a thing? Men true and constant! If it comes to that, I'll tell you that of all the men that I know, or have ever known, the best was my late husband. . . . I loved him passionately, with all my being, as none but a young, spiritual-minded woman can love; I gave him my youth, my life, my happiness, my fortune. He was the breath of my being, the idol I worshipped like a heathen, and—and that best of men deceived me in the most shameless fashion at every step! After his death I found in his table a drawer full of love-letters, and when he was alive—it is dreadful to remember!—he left me alone for weeks at a time. Before my very eyes he made love to other women and deceived me, squandered my money, mocked at my feelings. . . . And in spite of all that I loved him and was faithful to him. . . . What is more, I am still true and faithful to him. I have buried myself within four walls for ever, and I will not cast aside this mourning as long as I live.

SMIRNOV (*laughing contemptuously*). Mourning!

I don't know what you take me for. As though I don't know why you masquerade in black and shut yourself up within four walls! I should think so! It's so mysterious—so romantic! If some young ensign or unfledged poet passes your estate, he will look up at the windows and think, "Here lives the mysterious Tamara who from love for her husband has shut herself within four walls." I know all such tricks.

MADAME POPOV (*flushing crimson*). What? How dare you say such things to me!

SMIRNOV. You have buried yourself alive, but you have not forgotten to put powder on your face!

MADAME POPOV. How dare you speak to me like that!

SMIRNOV. Don't shout at me, please—I am not your steward! Allow me to call things by their real names. I am not a woman, and am accustomed to say what I think plainly. So don't shout, please.

MADAME POPOV. I am not shouting—it's you who shout. Kindly let me alone!

SMIRNOV. Pay me my money, and I will go away.

MADAME POPOV. I won't give you the money.

SMIRNOV. Yes, you will give it to me!

MADAME POPOV. Just to spite you, I won't give you a farthing! You may as well leave me in peace.

SMIRNOV. I haven't the pleasure of being married or engaged to you, and so please do not make a scene (*sits down*). I don't like it.

MADAME POPOV (*gasping with indignation*). You are sitting down?

SMIRNOV. I am.

MADAME POPOV. I beg you to go away.

SMIRNOV. Give me my money! (*Aside*) Oh, how furious I feel!

MADAME POPOV. I don't care to talk to insolent people. Be so good as to take yourself off (*a pause*). You won't go—you won't?

SMIRNOV. No.

MADAME POPOV. No?

SMIRNOV. No.

MADAME POPOV. Very good, then (*rings the bell*).

(*Enter* LUKA.)

MADAME POPOV. Luka, remove this gentleman.

LUKA (*approaches* SMIRNOV). Sir, kindly go when you are told. It's no use staying here——

SMIRNOV (*leaping up*). Hold your tongue! To whom are you speaking? I'll make mincemeat of you!

LUKA (*puts his hands on his heart*). Holy Saints! (*sinks into an armchair*). Oh, I feel ill! I feel ill! I can't breathe!

MADAME POPOV. Where's Dasha? Dasha! (*Shouts*) Dasha! Pelageya! Dasha! (*rings the bell*).

LUKA. Och! they've all gone to pick strawberries. There's no one in the house. I feel ill! Water!

MADAME POPOV. Kindly take yourself off.

SMIRNOV. Please be more polite.

MADAME POPOV (*clenching her fists and stamping*). You are a boor! A coarse bear! A bully! A monster!

SMIRNOV. What? What did you say?

MADAME POPOV. I said that you were a bear—a monster!

SMIRNOV (*stepping up to her*). Excuse me, what right have you to insult me?

MADAME POPOV. Yes, I am insulting you—what of it? Do you suppose I am afraid of you?

SMIRNOV. And do you think that because you are a poetical creature you have a right to insult people with impunity? Yes? I challenge you!

LUKA. Saints and holy martyrs! Water!

SMIRNOV. Pistols!

MADAME POPOV. If you have got strong fists and can bellow like a bull, do you think I am afraid of you, eh? You bully!

SMIRNOV. I challenge you! I allow no one to insult me, and it's nothing to me that you are a woman, a weak creature!

MADAME POPOV (*trying to shout him down*). Bear! bear! bear!

SMIRNOV. It's time to abandon the prejudice that only men must pay for an insult. If there is to be equality, then let it be equality. Damn it all! I challenge you!

MADAME POPOV. You want a duel? By all means!

SMIRNOV. This minute!

MADAME POPOV. This minute! My husband had pistols. . . . I'll fetch them at once (*goes out and hurriedly returns*). . . . What pleasure I shall have in putting a bullet through your brazen head! Damnation take you! (*goes out*).

SMIRNOV. I'll shoot her like a chicken! I am

not a boy, I am not a sentimental puppy—feminine frailty means nothing to me.

LUKA. My good gentleman (*drops on his knees*), for mercy's sake, have pity on an old man! Go away! You've frightened me to death, and now you are going to fight!

SMIRNOV (*not heeding him*). Fight a duel! That really is equality, emancipation! That does make the sexes equal! I shall shoot her on principle. But what a woman! (*Mimics her*) "Damnation take you! Put a bullet through your brazen head!" . . . What a woman! Her cheeks were flushed, her eyes sparkled. . . . She accepted the challenge! Honour bright, I've never seen anyone like her in my life! . . .

LUKA. Kind sir, go away! I'll remember you in my prayers!

SMIRNOV. She is something like a woman! I like that! A real woman! Not a mush of sentiment, but flame, gunpowder, fireworks! I shall be sorry to kill her.

LUKA (*weeps*). My good sir, go away!

SMIRNOV. I really like her. I really do! Though she has dimples in her cheeks, I like her! I would forgive her the debt even, and all my anger is gone. . . . A wonderful woman!

(*Enter* MADAME POPOV *with pistols.*)

MADAME POPOV. Here they are, the pistols. . . . But before we begin the duel, kindly show me how to fire. . . . I've never handled a pistol in my life.

LUKA. The Lord save us and have mercy upon us! I'll go and look for the gardener and the coachman. What's brought this trouble on us? (*goes out*).

SMIRNOV (*examining the pistols*). You see, there are several sorts of pistols. . . . There are special duelling pistols, the Mortimer pattern, with capsules. . . . But yours are the Smith-Wesson make, triple action with extractor. . . . They are fine pistols. They are worth at least ninety roubles the brace. . . . You have to hold the revolver like this. (*Aside*) What eyes! what eyes! A ravishing woman!

MADAME POPOV. Is that right?

SMIRNOV. Yes, that's it. . . . Then you raise the cock . . . take aim like this. . . . Throw your head a little back! . . . Stretch out your arm full length—that's it. . . . Then with this finger press on that little thing—and that's all. But the chief rule is not to get excited and to take aim slowly. Try not to let your hand shake.

MADAME POPOV. Very well. It's not convenient to fight indoors; let us go into the garden.

SMIRNOV. Let us. Only I warn you beforehand I shall fire into the air.

MADAME POPOV. That's the last straw! Why?

SMIRNOV. Because . . . because . . . that's my affair.

MADAME POPOV. You funk it, do you? A-a-ah! No, sir, no wriggling! Kindly follow me. I shall not be satisfied till I have put a bullet through your head—that head that's so hateful to me! Are you funking it?

SMIRNOV. Yes, I am.

MADAME POPOV. That's a lie. Why won't you fight?

SMIRNOV. Because . . . because . . . I like you.

MADAME POPOV (*with a malicious laugh*). He

likes me! He dares to say that he likes me! (*Pointing to the door*) You can go!

SMIRNOV (*in silence puts down the revolver, takes up his cap and is going; near the door he stops. For half a minute they look at each other in silence; then, going irresolutely towards* MADAME POPOV). I say—are you still angry? I, too, am devilish angry, but you know—how shall I put it? The fact is, you see—it's something like this, to put it plainly. (*Shouts*) Well, it's not my fault that I like you! (*Clutches at the back of the chair; the chair cracks and breaks*) Damnation, what fragile furniture you have! I like you. Do you understand? I—I am almost in love.

MADAME POPOV. Go away! I hate you!

SMIRNOV. Good God, what a woman! I have never seen anyone like her. I am lost! I am done for! I am caught like a mouse in a trap!

MADAME POPOV. Go away, or I'll fire.

SMIRNOV. Fire away! You can't imagine what joy it would be to die in the sight of those wonderful eyes—to be shot by a revolver held by that little velvety hand! . . . I have gone crazy! Think and decide at once, for if I go away from here, we shall never meet again. Decide! . . . I come of a good family, I am a gentleman, I have ten thousand roubles a year. . . . I can put a bullet through a halfpenny tossed in the air. . . . I've got first-rate horses. . . . Will you be my wife?

MADAME POPOV (*indignant, brandishes the revolver*). A duel! Let us fight!

SMIRNOV. I've gone crazy. I can't understand. (*Shouts*) Hi, there! Water!

MADAME POPOV (*shouts*). I challenge you!

SMIRNOV. I've gone crazy! I am in love like a boy—like a fool! (*Snatches her hand; she shrieks with pain*) I love you! (*Falls on his knees*) I love you as I have never loved before! I have thrown over twelve women, nine have thrown me over, but I never loved one of them as I love you. . . . I am getting maudlin, I am limp all over, I am a mush! Here I am on my knees like a fool and offering you my hand! . . . It's a shame, a disgrace! I've not been in love for five years. I vowed I wouldn't, and here I am completely bowled over! I offer you my hand. Yes or no? Won't you have it? Very well, you needn't! (*gets up and goes quickly to the door*).

MADAME POPOV. Stay!

SMIRNOV (*stopping*). Well?

MADAME POPOV. Nothing—go! But stay, though—no, go, go! I hate you! Oh, no!—don't go away! Oh, if you knew how angry I am! (*Throws the revolver on the table*) My fingers are numb from the horrid thing. (*Tears her handkerchief in a fury*) Why are you standing there? Go away!

SMIRNOV. Good-bye!

MADAME POPOV. Yes, yes, go away! (*Shouts*) Where are you going? Stay—you can go, though. Oh, how angry I feel! Don't come near me! Don't come near me!

SMIRNOV (*going up to her*). How angry I am with myself! I am in love like a schoolboy. I've been on my knees—it makes me feel cold all over. . . . (*Rudely*) I love you! As though I wanted to fall in love with you! To-morrow I have to pay my interest, the haymaking has begun, and now you on the top of it all. . . . (*Puts his arm round her waist*) I shall never forgive myself for this!

MADAME POPOV. Go away! Take your arms away! I—hate you! I chal—challenge you! (*A prolonged kiss.*)

(*Enter* LUKA *with an axe, the gardener with a rake, the coachman with a fork, and labourers with poles.*)

LUKA (*seeing the embracing couple*). Holy Saints!

(*A pause.*)

MADAME POPOV (*dropping her eyes*). Luka, teil them in the stable not to give Toby any oats to-day.

CURTAIN.

THE PROPOSAL

A JEST IN ONE ACT

First performed in 1889.

CHARACTERS IN THE PLAY

STEPAN STEPANOVITCH TCHUBUKOV (*a Landowner*).
NATALYA STEPANOVNA (*his daughter, aged* 25).
IVAN VASSILYEVITCH LOMOV (*a neighbour of* TCHUBUKOV'S, *a healthy, well-nourished, but hypochondriacal Landowner*).

THE PROPOSAL

A JEST IN ONE ACT

Drawing-room in TCHUBUKOV'S *house.* TCHUBUKOV *and* LOMOV; *the latter enters wearing evening dress and white gloves.*

TCHUBUKOV (*going to meet him*). My darling, whom do I see? Ivan Vassilyevitch! Delighted! (*shakes hands*). Well, this is a surprise, dearie. . . . How are you?

LOMOV. I thank you. And pray, how are you?

TCHUBUKOV. We are getting on all right, thanks to your prayers, my angel, and all the rest of it. Please sit down. . . . It's too bad, you know, to forget your neighbours, darling. But, my dear, why this ceremoniousness? A swallow-tail, gloves, and all the rest of it! Are you going visiting, my precious?

LOMOV. No, I have only come to see you, honoured Stepan Stepanovitch.

TCHUBUKOV. Then why the swallow-tail, my charmer? As though you were paying calls on New Year's Day!

LOMOV. You see, this is how it is (*takes his arm*). I have come, honoured Stepan Stepanovitch, to trouble you with a request. I have more than once had the honour of asking for your assistance, and you have always, so to speak—but pardon me,

I am agitated. I will have a drink of water, honoured Stepan Stepanovitch (*drinks water*).

TCHUBUKOV (*aside*). Come to ask for money! I am not going to give it to him. (*To him*) What is it, my beauty?

LOMOV. You see, Honour Stepanovitch—I beg your pardon, Stepan Honouritch. . . . I am dreadfully agitated, as you see. In short, no one but you can assist me, though, of course, I have done nothing to deserve it, and . . . and . . . have no right to reckon upon your assistance. . . .

TCHUBUKOV. Oh, don't spin it out, dearie. Come to the point. Well?

LOMOV. Immediately—in a moment. The fact is that I have come to ask for the hand of your daughter, Natalya Stepanovna.

TCHUBUKOV (*joyfully*). You precious darling! Ivan Vassilyevitch, say it again! I can't believe my ears.

LOMOV. I have the honour to ask . . .

TCHUBUKOV (*interrupting*). My darling! I am delighted, and all the rest of it. Yes, indeed, and all that sort of thing (*embraces and kisses him*). I have been hoping for it for ages. It has always been my wish (*sheds a tear*). And I have always loved you, my angel, as though you were my own son. God give you both love and good counsel, and all the rest of it. I have always wished for it. . . . Why am I standing here like a post? I am stupefied with joy, absolutely stupefied! Oh, from the bottom of my heart. . . . I'll go and call Natasha and that sort of thing.

LOMOV (*touched*). Honoured Stepan Stepanovitch, what do you think? May I hope that she will accept me?

TCHUBUKOV. A beauty like you, and she not accept you! I'll be bound she is as love-sick as a cat, and all the rest of it. . . . In a minute (*goes out*).

LOMOV. I am cold—I am trembling all over, as though I were in for an examination. The great thing is to make up one's mind. If one thinks about it too long, hesitates, discusses it, waits for one's ideal or for real love, one will never get married. . . . Brr! I am cold. Natalya Stepanovna is an excellent manager, not bad looking, educated—what more do I want? But I am beginning to have noises in my head. I am so upset (*sips water*). And get married I must. To begin with, I am thirty-five—a critical age, so to speak. And, secondly, I need a regular, well-ordered life. . . . I have valvular disease of the heart, continual palpitations. I am hasty, and am very easily upset. . . . Now, for instance, my lips are quivering and my right eyelid is twitching. . . . But my worst trouble is with sleep. No sooner have I got into bed and just begun to drop asleep, than I have a shooting pain in my left side and a stabbing at my shoulder and my head. . . . I leap up like a madman. I walk about a little and lie down again, but no sooner do I drop off than there's the shooting pain in my side again. And the same thing twenty times over! . . .

(*Enter* NATALYA STEPANOVNA.)

NATALYA. Well, so it's you! Why, and papa said a purchaser had come for the goods! How do you do, Ivan Vassilyevitch?

LOMOV. How do you do, honoured Natalya Stepanovna!

NATALYA. Excuse my apron and *négligé*. We are shelling peas for drying. How is it you have not been to see us for so long? Sit down. (*They sit down.*) Will you have some lunch?

LOMOV. No, thank you, I have already lunched.

NATALYA. Won't you smoke? Here are the matches. . . . It's a magnificent day, but yesterday it rained so hard that the men did no work at all. How many hay-cocks have you got out? Only fancy, I have been too eager and had the whole meadow mown, and now I am sorry—I am afraid the hay will rot. It would have been better to wait. But what's this? I do believe you have got on your dress-coat! That's something new. Are you going to a ball, or what? And, by the way, you are looking nice. . . . Why are you such a swell, really?

LOMOV (*in agitation*). You see, honoured Natalya Stepanovna. . . . The fact is that I have made up my mind to ask you to listen to me. . . . Of course, you will be surprised, and even angry, but I . . . It's horribly cold!

NATALYA. What is it? (*a pause*). Well?

LOMOV. I will try to be brief. You are aware, honoured Natalya Stepanovna, that from my earliest childhood I had the honour of knowing your family. My late aunt and her husband, from whom, as you know, I inherited the estate, always entertained a profound respect for your papa and your late mamma. The family of the Lomovs and the family of the Tchubukovs have always been on the most friendly and, one may say, intimate terms. Moreover, as you are aware, my land is in close proximity to yours. If you remember, my Volovyi meadows are bounded by your birch copse.

NATALYA. Excuse my interrupting you. You say "*my* Volovyi meadows." . . . But are they yours?

LOMOV. Yes, mine.

NATALYA. Well, what next! The Volovyi meadows are ours, not yours!

LOMOV. No, they are mine, honoured Natalya Stepanovna.

NATALYA. That's news to me. How do they come to be yours?

LOMOV. How do they come to be mine? I am speaking of the Volovyi meadows that run like a wedge between your birch copse and the Charred Swamp.

NATALYA. Quite so. Those are ours.

LOMOV. No, you are mistaken, honoured Natalya Stepanovna, they are mine.

NATALYA. Think what you are saying, Ivan Vassilyevitch! Have they been yours long?

LOMOV. What do you mean by "long"? As long as I can remember they have always been ours.

NATALYA. Well, there you must excuse me.

LOMOV. There is documentary evidence for it, honoured Natalya Stepanovna. The Volovyi meadows were once a matter of dispute, that is true, but now everyone knows that they are mine. And there can be no dispute about it. Kindly consider . . . my aunt's grandmother gave over those meadows to the peasants of your father's grandfather for their use, rent free, for an indefinite period, in return for their firing her bricks. The peasants of your father's grandfather enjoyed the use of the meadows, rent free, for some forty years, and grew used to looking upon them as their own; afterwards, when the settlement came about after the emancipation . . .

NATALYA. It is not at all as you say! Both my grandfather and my great-grandfather considered their land reached to the Charred Swamp—so the Volovyi meadows were ours. I can't understand what there is to argue about. It's really annoying!

LOMOV. I will show you documents, Natalya Stepanovna.

NATALYA. No, you are simply joking, or trying to tease me. . . . A nice sort of surprise! We have owned the land nearly three hundred years, and all of a sudden we are told that the land is not ours! Forgive me, Ivan Vassilyevitch, but I positively cannot believe my ears. . . . I don't care about the meadows. They are not more than fifteen acres, and they are only worth some three hundred roubles, but I am revolted by injustice. You may say what you like, but I cannot endure injustice!

LOMOV. Listen to me, I implore you. The peasants of your father's grandfather, as I had already the honour to inform you, made bricks for my aunt's grandmother. My aunt's grandmother, wishing to do something for them . . .

NATALYA. Grandfather, grandmother, aunt. . . .

I don't understand a word of it. The meadows are ours, and that's all about it.

LOMOV. They are mine.

NATALYA. They are ours. If you go on arguing for two days, if you put on fifteen dress coats, they are still ours, ours, ours! . . . I don't want what's yours, but I don't want to lose what's mine. . . . You can take that as you please!

LOMOV. I do not care about the meadows, Natalya Stepanovna, but it is a matter of principle. If you like, I will make you a present of them.

NATALYA. I might make you a present of them, they are mine. All this is very queer, Ivan Vassilyevitch, to say the least of it. Hitherto we have looked upon you as a good neighbour—a friend. Last year we lent you our threshing-machine, and through that we couldn't finish our threshing till November; and you treat us as if we were gipsies! Make me a present of my own land! Excuse me, but that is not neighbourly. To my thinking it is positively impertinent, if you care to know. . . .

LOMOV. According to you I am a usurper, then? I've never snatched other people's land, madam, and I will allow no one to accuse me of such a thing . . . (*goes rapidly to the decanter and drinks water*). The Volovyi meadows are mine!

NATALYA. It's not true: they are ours!

LOMOV. They are mine!

NATALYA. That's not true. I'll prove it. I'll send our mowers to cut the hay there to-day!

LOMOV. What?

NATALYA. My labourers will be there to-day.

LOMOV. I'll kick them out.

NATALYA. Don't you dare!

LOMOV (*clutches at his heart*). The Volovyi meadows are mine! Do you understand? Mine!

NATALYA. Don't shout, please. You can shout and choke with rage when you are at home, if you like; but here I beg you to keep within bounds.

LOMOV. If it were not for these terrible, agonising palpitations, madam—if it were not for the throbbing in my temples, I should speak to you very differently. (*Shouts*) The Volovyi meadows are mine!

NATALYA. Ours!

LOMOV. Mine!

NATALYA. Ours!

LOMOV. Mine!

(*Enter* TCHUBUKOV.)

TCHUBUKOV. What is it? What are you shouting about?

NATALYA. Papa, explain to this gentleman, please: to whom do the Volovyi meadows belong—to him or to us?

TCHUBUKOV (*to* LOMOV). My chicken, the meadows are ours.

LOMOV. But upon my word, Stepan Stepanovitch, how did they come to be yours? Do you, at least, be reasonable. My aunt's grandmother gave over the meadows for temporary gratuitous use to your grandfather's peasants. The peasants made use of the land for forty years and got used to regarding it as their own; but when the Settlement came . . .

TCHUBUKOV. Allow me, my precious. . . . You

forget that the peasants did not pay your grandmother rent and all the rest of it, just because the ownership of the land was in dispute, and so on. . . . And now every dog knows that they are ours. You can't have seen the map.

LOMOV. I will prove to you that they are mine.

TCHUBUKOV. You never will, my pet.

LOMOV. Yes, I will.

TCHUBUKOV. Why are you shouting, my love? You will prove nothing at all by shouting. I don't desire what is yours, and don't intend to give up what is mine. Why ever should I? If it comes to that, my dear, if you intend to wrangle over the meadows, I would rather give them to the peasants than to you, that I would!

LOMOV. I don't understand it. What right have you to give away another man's property?

TCHUBUKOV. Allow me to decide for myself whether I have the right or no. I may say, young man, I am not accustomed to being spoken to in that tone, and all the rest of it. I am twice as old as you are, young man, and I beg you to speak to me without getting excited and all the rest of it.

LOMOV. Why, you simply take me for a fool and are laughing at me! You call my land yours, and then you expect me to be cool about it and to speak to you properly! That's not the way good neighbours behave, Stepan Stepanovitch. You are not a neighbour, but a usurper!

TCHUBUKOV. What? What did you say?

NATALYA. Papa, send the men at once to mow the meadows.

TCHUBUKOV (*to* LOMOV). What did you say, sir?

NATALYA. The Volovyi meadows are ours, and I won't give them up. I won't! I won't!

LOMOV. We will see about that. I'll prove to you in court that they are mine.

TCHUBUKOV. In court? You can take it into court, sir, and all the rest of it! You can! I know you—you are only waiting for a chance to go to law, and so on. . . . A pettifogging character! All your family were fond of litigation—all of them!

LOMOV. I beg you not to insult my family. The Lomovs have all been honest men, and not one of them has ever been on his trial for embezzling money like your uncle!

TCHUBUKOV. Well, you Lomovs have all been mad!

NATALYA. Everyone of them — everyone of them!

TCHUBUKOV. Your grandfather was a dipsomaniac, and your youngest aunt, Nastasya Mihailovna, ran away with an architect, and so on.

LOMOV. And your mother was a hunchback (*clutches at his heart*). The shooting pain in my side! . . . The blood has rushed to my head. . . . Holy Saints! . . . Water!

TCHUBUKOV. And your father was a gambler and a glutton!

NATALYA. And there was no one like your aunt for talking scandal!

LOMOV. My left leg has all gone numb. . . . And you are an intriguer! . . . Oh, my heart! . . . And it is no secret that before the elections you . . . There are flashes before my eyes! . . . Where is my hat?

NATALYA. It's mean! It's dishonest! It's disgusting!

TCHUBUKOV. And you yourself are a viperish, double-faced, mischief-making man. Yes, indeed!

LOMOV. Here is my hat. . . . My heart! . . . Which way am I to go? Where's the door? Oh! I believe I am dying. I've lost the use of my leg (*goes towards the door*).

TCHUBUKOV (*calling after him*). Never set foot within my door again!

NATALYA. Take it into court! We shall see!

(LOMOV *goes out, staggering.*)

TCHUBUKOV. Damnation take him! (*walks about in excitement*).

NATALYA. What a wretch! How is one to believe in good neighbours after that!

TCHUBUKOV. Blackguard! Scarecrow!

NATALYA. The object! Collars other people's land—then abuses them!

TCHUBUKOV. And that noodle—that eyesore—had the face to make a proposal, and all the rest of it. Just fancy, a proposal!

NATALYA. What proposal?

TCHUBUKOV. Why, he came here on purpose to propose to you!

NATALYA. To propose? To me? Why didn't you tell me so before?

TCHUBUKOV. And he had got himself up in his dress coat on purpose! The sausage! The shrimp!

NATALYA. To me? A proposal! Ah! (*She falls into an armchair and moans*) Bring him back! Bring him back! Oh, bring him back!

TCHUBUKOV. Bring whom back?

NATALYA. Make haste, make haste! I feel faint! Bring him back! (*Hysterics.*)

TCHUBUKOV. What is it! What's the matter? (*clutches at his head*). I do have a life of it! I shall shoot myself! I shall hang myself! They'll be the death of me!

NATALYA. I am dying! Bring him back!

TCHUBUKOV. Tfoo! Directly. Don't howl (*runs off*).

NATALYA (*alone, moans*). What have we done! Bring him back! Bring him back!

TCHUBUKOV (*runs in*). He is just coming in, and all the rest of it. Damnation take him! Ough! Talk to him yourself, I don't want to. . . .

NATALYA (*moans*). Bring him back!

TCHUBUKOV (*shouts*). He is coming, I tell you! What a task it is, O Lord, to be the father of a grown-up daughter! I shall cut my throat! I shall certainly cut my throat! We've abused the man, put him to shame, kicked him out, and it is all your doing—your doing!

NATALYA. No, it was yours!

TCHUBUKOV. Oh, it's my fault, so that's it! (LOMOV *appears at the door*). Well, talk to him yourself (*goes out*).

(*Enter* LOMOV *in a state of collapse.*)

LOMOV. Fearful palpitations! My leg is numb . . . there's a stitch in my side. . . .

NATALYA. Forgive us; we were too hasty, Ivan Vassilyevitch. I remember now: the Volovyi meadows really are yours.

LOMOV. My heart is throbbing frightfully. . . .

The meadows are mine. . . . There's a twitching in both my eyelids.

NATALYA. Yes, they are yours, they are. Sit down. (*They sit down.*) We were wrong.

LOMOV. I acted from principle. . . . I do not value the land, but I value the principle. . . .

NATALYA. Just so, the principle. . . . Let us talk of something else.

LOMOV. Especially as I have proofs. My aunt's grandmother gave the peasants of your father's grandfather . . .

NATALYA. Enough, enough about that. . . . (*Aside*) I don't know how to begin. (*To him*) Shall you soon be going shooting ?

LOMOV. I expect to go grouse shooting after the harvest, honoured Natalya Stepanovna. Oh ! did you hear ? Only fancy, I had such a misfortune ! My Tracker, whom I think you know, has fallen lame.

NATALYA. What a pity ! How did it happen ?

LOMOV. I don't know. . . . He must have put his paw out of joint, or perhaps some other dog bit it. . . . (*Sighs*) My very best dog, to say nothing of the money I have spent on him ! You know I paid Mironov a hundred and twenty-five roubles for him.

NATALYA. You gave too much, Ivan Vassilyevitch !

LOMOV. Well, to my mind it was very cheap. He is a delightful dog.

NATALYA. Father gave eighty-five roubles for his Backer, and Backer is a much better dog than your Tracker.

LOMOV. Backer a better dog than Tracker? What nonsense! (*laughs*). Backer a better dog than Tracker!

NATALYA. Of course he is better. It's true that Backer is young yet—he is hardly a full-grown dog—but for points and cleverness even Voltchanetsky hasn't one to beat him.

LOMOV. Excuse me, Natalya Stepanovna, but you forget that your Backer has a pug-jaw, and a dog with a pug-jaw is never any good for gripping.

NATALYA. A pug-jaw! That's the first time I've heard so.

LOMOV. I assure you the lower jaw is shorter than the upper.

NATALYA. Why, have you measured?

LOMOV. Yes. He is all right for coursing, no doubt, but for gripping he'd hardly do.

NATALYA. In the first place, our Backer is a pedigree dog, son of Harness and Chisel, but you can't even tell what breed your spotty piebald is. . . . Then he is as old and ugly as a broken-down horse.

LOMOV. He is old, but I wouldn't exchange him for half a dozen of your Backers. . . . How could I? Tracker is a dog, but Backer—there can be no question about it. Every huntsman has packs and packs of dogs like your Backer. Twenty-five roubles would be a good price for him.

NATALYA. There is a demon of contradictoriness in you to-day, Ivan Vassilyevitch. First you make out that the meadows are yours, then that your Tracker is a better dog than Backer. I don't like a man to say what he does not think.

You know perfectly well that Backer is worth a hundred of your . . . stupid Trackers. Why, then, say the opposite?

LOMOV. I see, Natalya Stepanovna, that you think I am blind or a fool. Do understand that your Backer has a pug-jaw?

NATALYA. It's not true!

LOMOV. It is!

NATALYA (*shouts*). It's not true!

LOMOV. Why are you shouting, madam?

NATALYA. Why do you talk nonsense? This is revolting! It's time your Tracker was shot—and you compare him to Backer!

LOMOV. Excuse me, I cannot continue this argument. I have palpitations.

NATALYA. I have noticed that men argue most about hunting who know least about it.

LOMOV. Madam, I beg you to be silent. My heart is bursting. (*Shouts*) Be silent!

NATALYA. I will not be silent till you own that Backer is a hundred times better than your Tracker.

LOMOV. A hundred times worse! Plague take your Backer! My temples . . . my eyes . . . my shoulder. . . .

NATALYA. There's no need for plague to take your fool of a Tracker—he is as good as dead already.

LOMOV (*weeping*). Be silent! My heart is bursting!

NATALYA. I won't be silent.

(*Enter* TCHUBUKOV.)

TCHUBUKOV (*coming in*). What now?

NATALYA. Papa, tell me truly, on your conscience, which is the better dog—our Backer or his Tracker?

LOMOV. Stepan Stepanovitch, I implore you tell me one thing only: has your Backer a pug-jaw or not? Yes or no?

TCHUBUKOV. And what if he has? It's of no consequence. Anyway, there's no better dog in the whole district, and all the rest of it.

LOMOV. But my Tracker is better, isn't he? Honestly?

TCHUBUKOV. Don't excite yourself, my precious. Your Tracker certainly has his good qualities. . . . He is a well-bred dog, has good legs, and is well set-up, and all the rest of it. But the dog, if you care to know, my beauty, has two serious defects: he is old and is snub-nosed.

LOMOV. Excuse me, I have palpitations. . . . Let us take the facts. . . . If you will kindly remember, at Maruskin's my Tracker kept shoulder to shoulder with the Count's Swinger, while your Backer was a good half-mile behind.

TCHUBUKOV. Yes, he was, because the Count's huntsman gave him a crack with his whip.

LOMOV. He deserved it. All the other dogs were after the fox, but Backer got hold of a sheep.

TCHUBUKOV. That's not true! . . . Darling, I am hot-tempered, and I beg you to drop this conversation. He lashed him because everyone is jealous of another man's dog. . . . Yes, they are all envious! And you are not free from blame on that score either, sir. As soon as you notice, for instance, that someone's dog is better than your Tracker, at once you begin with this and that, and all the rest of it. I remember it all!

LOMOV. I remember it too!

TCHUBUKOV (*mimics him*). "I remember it too!" And what do you remember?

LOMOV. Palpitations! . . . My leg has no feeling in it. I can't . . .

NATALYA (*mimicking him*). "Palpitations!" . . . A fine sportsman! You ought to be lying on the stove in the kitchen squashing blackbeetles instead of hunting foxes. Palpitations!

TCHUBUKOV. Yes, you are a fine sportsman, really! With your palpitations you ought to stay at home, instead of jolting in the saddle. It wouldn't matter if you hunted, but you only ride out to wrangle and interfere with other men's dogs and all the rest of it. I am hot-tempered; let us drop this subject. You are not a sportsman at all.

LOMOV. And you—are you a sportsman? You only go to the hunt to intrigue and make up to the Count. . . . My heart! . . . You are an intriguer!

TCHUBUKOV. What? Me an intriguer? (*Shouts*) Hold your tongue!

LOMOV. Intriguer!

TCHUBUKOV. Milksop! Puppy!

LOMOV. Old rat! Jesuit!

TCHUBUKOV. Hold your tongue, or I'll shoot you with a filthy gun like a partridge! Noodle!

LOMOV. Everyone knows—oh, my heart!—that your wife used to beat you. . . . My leg . . . my forehead . . . my eyes! . . . I shall drop! I shall drop!

TCHUBUKOV. And you go in terror of your housekeeper!

LOMOV. Oh, oh, oh! My heart has burst! I can't feel my shoulder—what has become of my shoulder? I am dying! (*falls into an armchair*). A doctor! (*swoons*).

TCHUBUKOV. Puppy! Milksop! Noodle! I feel faint! (*drinks water*). Faint!

NATALYA. You are a fine sportsman! You don't know how to sit on your horse. (*To her father*) Papa, what's the matter with him? Papa! Look, papa! (*shrieks*). Ivan Vassilyevitch! He is dead!

TCHUBUKOV. I feel faint! I can't breathe! Give me air!

NATALYA. He is dead! (*shakes* LOMOV *by the sleeve*). Ivan Vassilyevitch! Ivan Vassilyevitch! What have we done! He is dead! (*falls into an armchair*). A doctor! a doctor! (*hysterics*).

TCHUBUKOV. Och! What is it? What do you want?

NATALYA (*moans*). He is dead! He is dead!

TCHUBUKOV. Who is dead? (*looking at* LOMOV) He really is dead! Holy Saints! Water! A doctor! (*Holds a glass of water to* LOMOV'S *lips*) Drink! . . . No, he won't drink. So he is dead, and all the rest of it. I do have a life of it! Why don't I put a bullet through my brains? Why is it I haven't cut my throat? What am I waiting for? Give me a knife! Give me a pistol! (LOMOV *makes a slight movement.*) I believe he is reviving. . . . Have a drink of water. That's right.

LOMOV. Flashes—dizziness—where am I ?

TCHUBUKOV. You'd better make haste and get married—and go to the devil ! She consents (*joins the hands of* LOMOV *and his daughter*). She accepts you, and all the rest of it. I give you my blessing, and so on. Only leave me in peace.

LOMOV. Eh ? What ? (*getting up*). Who ?

TCHUBUKOV. She accepts you. Well ? Kiss each other and . . . be damned to you !

NATALYA (*moans*). He is alive ! Yes, yes, I accept.

TCHUBUKOV. Kiss !

LOMOV. Eh ? Whom ? (*kisses* NATALYA STEPANOVNA). Delighted ! Excuse me, what's the point ? Oh, yes, I understand ! Palpitations . . . dizziness . . . I am happy, Natalya Stepanovna (*kisses her hand*). My leg is numb !

NATALYA. I . . . I too am happy.

TCHUBUKOV. It's a load off my heart ! Ough !

NATALYA. But . . . still you must admit now that Tracker is not as good a dog as Backer.

LOMOV. He is better !

NATALYA. He is worse !

TCHUBUKOV. Well, here's the beginning of family happiness ! Champagne !

LOMOV. He is better !

NATALYA. He is not ! He is not ! He is not !

TCHUBUKOV (*trying to shout them down*). Champagne ! Champagne !

CURTAIN.

You are mine . . . mine. . . . This forehead is mine, and these eyes, and this lovely silky hair is mine too . . . you are mine all over. You are so gifted, so clever, the best of all modern writers, you are the one hope of Russia. . . . You have so much truthfulness, simplicity, freshness, healthy humour. . . . In one touch you can give all the essential characteristics of a person or a landscape, your characters are living. One can't read you without delight! You think this is exaggerated? That I am flattering you? But look into my eyes . . . look. . . . Do I look like a liar? You see, I am the only one who can appreciate you; I am the only one who tells you the truth, my precious, wonderful darling. . . . Are you coming? Yes? You won't abandon me? . . .

TRIGORIN. I have no will of my own . . . I have never had a will of my own. . . . Flabby, feeble, always submissive—how can a woman care for such a man? Take me, carry me off, but don't let me move a step away from you. . . .

MADAME ARKADIN (*to herself*). Now he is mine! (*In an easy tone as though nothing had happened*) But, of course, if you like, you can stay. I'll go by myself and you can come afterwards, a week later. After all, why should you be in a hurry?

TRIGORIN. No, we may as well go together.

MADAME ARKADIN. As you please. Let us go together then (*a pause*).

(TRIGORIN *makes a note.*)

MADAME ARKADIN. What are you writing?

TRIGORIN. I heard a good name this morning,

an ordinary woman, you can't talk like that to me. Don't torture me, Boris. It terrifies me.

TRIGORIN. If you cared to, you could be not ordinary. Love—youthful, charming, poetical, lifting one into a world of dreams—that's the only thing in life that can give happiness! I have never yet known a love like that. . . . In my youth I never had time, I was always hanging about the editors' offices, struggling with want. Now it is here, that love, it has come, it beckons to me. What sense is there in running away from it?

MADAME ARKADIN (*wrathfully*). You have gone mad!

TRIGORIN. Well, let me?

MADAME ARKADIN. You are all in a conspiracy together to torment me to-day! (*weeps*).

TRIGORIN (*clutching at his heart*). She does not understand! She won't understand!

MADAME ARKADIN. Am I so old and ugly that you don't mind talking of other women to me? (*puts her arms round him and kisses him*). Oh, you are mad! My wonderful, splendid darling. . . . You are the last page of my life! (*falls on her knees*). My joy, my pride, my bliss! . . . (*embraces his knees*). If you forsake me even for one hour I shall not survive it, I shall go mad, my marvellous, magnificent one, my master. . . .

TRIGORIN. Someone may come in (*helps her to get up*).

MADAME ARKADIN. Let them, I am not ashamed of my love for you (*kisses his hands*). My treasure, you desperate boy, you want to be mad, but I won't have it, I won't let you . . . (*laughs*).